MASTER
TEACHER

BY Edward Kuhlman:

An Overwhelming Interference

Master Teacher

MASTER TEACHER

EDWARD KUHLMAN

Fleming H. Revell Company
Old Tappan, New Jersey

Scripture quotations are from the King James Version of the Bible.

Quotations from *Great Teachers: As Portrayed by those Who Studied Under Them*, edited by Houston Peterson, Rutgers University Press, New Brunswick, New Jersey, 1946.

Material reprinted with permission of Macmillan Publishing Company from UNSEEN HARVESTS: A TREASURY OF TEACHING by Claude Moore Fuess and Emory S. Basford. Copyright © 1947 by Macmillan Publishing Company, renewed 1975 by Claude Moore Fuess and Emory S. Basford.

Extract from THE SKY IS RED by Geoffrey Bull (Pickering & Inglis) reprinted by permission of Marshall Pickering, Basingstroke.

Quotation from "Accepted in the Beloved" by Civilla D. Martin. Copyright 1930. Renewal 1958 by Hope Publishing Co., Carol Stream, IL 60188. Used by Permission.

Letter on page 26 used by permission of Pamela C. Jensen.

"A Sort of Song," William Carlos Williams, *COLLECTED LATER POEMS*. Copyright 1948 by William Carlos Williams. Reprinted by permission of New Directions Publishing Corporation.

Quotations from OLD SCHOOL-DAY ROMANCES by James Whitcomb Riley (Indianapolis: Bobbs-Merrill, 1909).

"Cipher in the Snow" by Jean Mizer, NEA Journal, National Education Association.

"DeCiphered," by Edward Kuhlman, from *The Personnel and Guidance Journal* © AACD. Reproduced with permission. No further reproduction authorized without written permission of AACD.

Library of Congress Cataloging-in-Publication Data
Kuhlman, Edward.
    Master teacher.

    Bibliography:
    1. Jesus Christ—Teaching methods.   I. Title.
BT590.T5K85   1987   232.9'04   87-4820
ISBN 0-8007-1536-5

With heartfelt thanks to all the teachers and students
who have enriched my life along the way
but especially

TO

Mitch and Jane,

who have taught me and many others
about the love of Christ

CONTENTS

CONTENTS

INTRODUCTION: THE GOOD TEACHER

A long time ago, they tell us, Zeus assembled around him all men to give immortality to the one having done the worthiest deed. One by one they came forward, recounting their deeds of valor and distinction, till only a kindly old man was left. "And what is it *you* have done?" inquired Zeus. "I am a teacher," he replied, "and all these men here before you were my pupils." Then spoke Zeus: "Thou art the greatest among men and deserving immortality before all others."[1]

INTRODUCTION

A Lifetime to Learn In

From birth to death, we all learn, and the more effectively we learn, the more effectively we live. Our whole lives become influenced by our lessons and teachers, and in great part, our personality differences result from the variations in them. We have learned how to act and have become what others have taught us to be. Although we inherit temperamental predispositions and our genetic endowments, if no one had taught us to make our way in the world, we could not have survived. It's that simple.

Fascinating studies dealing with feral children support the belief that to be "human" means, in a significant sense, that we have learned human ways, ideas, and behavior. John Locke may have been close to the truth when he told us, "The difference to be found in the manners and abilities of men is owing more to their education than anything else."[2]

All through life, people help us learn. Some teachers carry a formal title and function in professional roles in schools, colleges, churches, and other institutions. But a host of others teach us informally, as well. First we encounter the lessons from our parents (or their substitutes). As they guide us through the "primer days" of childhood their instruction marks us indelibly. By imitating them, we learn to talk. We mimic their mannerisms. We internalize much of their value systems. Homes are educative places; throughout life we cherish what we have learned to value there.

My wife and I dutifully assigned highest priority to our responsibility for "parental pedagogy," seeking to teach our children both by example and word. Because we wanted them to appreciate the value of literature, books abounded in our home.

Each night, before bedtime, we faithfully read to our three children, and my oldest daughter still grimaces when she recalls the soliloquies from Shakespeare (especially from *Macbeth*) recited to her at bathtime. Music was very much a part of our family life, and those early selections that our children heard continue to shape their musical preferences.

Beyond the Home

As a child's life expands, opportunites to learn from other sources widen, too. Beyond his own door, new worlds open to him.

Apart from the home, few agencies have paralleled the Sunday school in the religious instruction of children. Originally established in Great Britain, to provide schooling for indigent and illiterate children, who otherwise would have been unable to learn to read and write, the Sunday school has become a place where godly teachers now teach children about the love of Christ. Over time the purpose of such schools has changed, and Christian education has replaced literacy education. Though these programs now focus upon lessons in Scripture and moral development, the influence of consecrated teachers has never lessened. We could assemble voluminous tributes to the faithful (if not famous) Sunday-school teachers. If we erected a Sunday-school teachers' hall of fame, we no doubt would enshrine there J. W. T. Dewhirst of Yorkshire, England. To one of his pupils Dewhirst said: "I had always hoped that you would go into the ministry." Because of Dewhirst's prompting, that boy became a minister and "the greatest preacher in the English-speaking world. His name was John Henry Jowett."[3]

The hall of fame would include a citation to the anonymous teacher who led the great London preacher Joseph Parker to Christ; as well as a tribute to James Kennedy, who encouraged Scotland's great preacher Alexander Whyte. Certainly a special place similar to the Poets' Corner in Westminster Abbey would be reserved for Edward Kimball, the teacher who gave his time to a seemingly unpromising youth who became renowned evangelist Dwight L. Moody.

Influential Teachers

Teachers come into our lives from various sources. Children learn from parents, parents occasionally from children; wives from husbands, and husbands from wives. From such myriad incidental contacts we all learn. However, when we think of the word *teacher,* typically we also think of schools we attended, the desks in which we sat, the chalkboards we faced, the lessons we worked on, and the people who formally held that title. For better or worse, they taught us much. Some we revere with a devotion bordering on worship; others, we would just as happily forget. Sifting through the strata of our educational lives, we find these people played decisive, prominent roles in our lives. Much of what and who we are is because of who they were.

Prize-winning novelist Thomas Wolfe paid one of the most stirring tributes to a teacher. That acknowledged master of descriptive prose wrote the following letter of gratitude and indebtedness for his teacher, Mrs. Roberts, when school officials challenged her teaching credentials.

My friend and former teacher, Mrs. J. M. Roberts, has lately written me explaining that some testimonial is desired as to her quality as a teacher and asking me if I would care to record any opinion I have on that subject. I esteem it an honor and a privilege to do this, although I find myself in constant difficulties when I try to keep my pen from leaping away with a red-hot panegyric.

. . . I can do no less than consider Mrs. Roberts as one of the three great teachers who have ever taught me,—this with all honor to Harvard, who has not yet succeeded in adding a fourth name to my own Hall of Fame. More than anyone else I have ever known, Mrs. Roberts succeeded in getting under my skull with an appreciation of what is fine and altogether worthwhile in literature. That, in my opinion, is the vital quality. That is the essential thing—the mark of a real teacher.

13

. . . During the years Mrs. Roberts taught me she exercised an influence that is inestimable on almost every particular of my life and thought. With the other boys of my age I know she did the same. We turned instinctively to this lady for her advice and direction and we trusted it unfalteringly.

I think that kind of relation is one of the profoundest experiences of anyone's life,—I put the relation of a fine teacher to a student just below the relation of a mother to her son and I don't think I could say more than this.

You can readily understand that the intimacy of such a relation is much more important in those formative years at grammar school or high school. . . . The point is that I did get it at a time when it was supremely important that I get it. It is, therefore, impossible that I ever forget the influence of Mrs. Roberts. She is one of my great people, and happy are those who can claim her as their teacher.[4]

Winston Churchill, whose oratory and unrivaled command of the English language inspired the British people to victory during World War II, has identified and praised the teachers who inspired him.

But I was taught English. Mr. Somervell—a delightful man, to whom my debt is great—was charged with the duty of teaching the stupidest boys the most disregarded thing—namely, to write mere English. He knew how to do it. He taught it as no one else has ever taught it. . . . Thus I got into my bones the essential structure of the ordinary British sentence—which is a noble thing.[5]

Mr. Moriarity, greatly beloved by all students and colleagues at Harrow, was probably "the master who had the greatest influence on Winston Churchill's future career." That man of "impeccable teaching skill . . . was possessed by a gracious manner and such charm . . . that the glacial distinctions melted away and the springs of friendliness were soon apparent. . . ." After Churchill left Harrow, he kept up a regular correspondence with his former teacher, always signing his letters: "Your affectionate pupil." In response to Moriarity's congratulatory letter, when Churchill was named to a high position in the British government, the politician wrote: "Almost the only valuable and pleasant part of my instruction there was received at your hands, and though I fear I am sadly lacking in scholarly education, the taste for history which I acquired or developed in your Army class has been pleasantly indulged by me in the years that are past."[6]

Identifying the "Good Teacher"

What makes a good teacher? The massive professional research literature on this question provides no conclusive answers. Consensus concerning the elements of effective teaching is lacking; we cannot unerringly identify the sine qua non of the quality teacher. However, we still know a *good teacher* when we see one.

All this seems to imply that we can associate a number of characteristics with good teachers. Temperament, personality, style, interaction, communication skills, and even the elusive factor called charisma all have their part. Although history has celebrated teachers who have touched the lives of their students and who have been noted for educational excellence, no single individual can stake claim to the title of *the* master-teacher—the teacher par excellence. Even Socrates, the revered teacher of Plato, does not make the grade by today's standards. Among human teachers, we fail to find one who has become the standard by which we judge all others. However, when we look at the One "sent from God," we come face-to-face with *the* Teacher who excels all others and defines within Himself for all time what a teacher is.

This book is an encounter with *that* Teacher. I have written from the practicing teacher's point of view, with today's schools in mind. I've not attempted an analysis of our Lord Jesus Christ, nor have I attempted, per se, to scrutinize His teaching techniques, although we'll look at them. It is not a prescription for academicians to utilize in their educational activities, and certainly it is not a "tips for teachers" talk. Instead I conceived the book as a meditation upon the Master-Teacher. I propose a devotional, reverent reflection of Him who came to teach us about God. This is one teacher's talk about the supremely qualified Teacher of teachers who has come among us, who talks truth and is Truth (John 14:6).

MASTER TEACHER

— Part I —
WHERE
LEARNING
BEGINS

It all starts in a wonderful, mystical experience that begins on a path lined with books and teachers—both the good and not-so-good ones.

Join me on a journey of heart, mind, and soul.

1
CALL ME TEACHER

. . .Yet shall not thy teachers be removed into a corner any more, but thine eyes shall see thy teachers.

Isaiah 30:20

The most important day I remember in all my life is the one on which my teacher, Anne M. Sullivan, came to me. I am filled with wonder when I consider the immeasurable contrast between the two lives which it connects.[1]

Mr. Alfred Twistead was a teacher. . . . He had been doing this for nearly forty years. . . . As the time for his retirement drew near, Mr. Twistead became very excited. . . . He had planned what he was going to do with his leisure when it came to him. There was a lot that needed doing . . . altogether plenty of ways of filling up his time. . . .

And tears came into his eyes as he thought of the weary struggle it had all been. . . .

Mr. Twistead was in the habit of getting up in the morning to make an early cup of tea. His wife smiled when she noticed that the next morning he did not stir, remembering how unnecessary it was now for him to be up in good time. Then she saw something peculiar in the way he was lying, and touched him and found him cold, and began to cry quietly; for he was dead.[2]

Herman Melville begins his celebrated novel *Moby Dick* with the words "Call me Ishmael."[3] Kurt Vonnegut, Jr., not to be outdone, commences *Cat's Cradle* with: "Call me Jonah."[4] Without my making any claim of following in their literary lineage, you can "call me teacher." That's my trade. I've been at it for a quarter of a century. I have also watched teachers, in one school or another, for years.

Teachers have had an important place in my life; a long line of them paraded down my educational paths. At first I think about those who majored in the tried and trite—the ones Gilbert Highet called "gloomy routinists."[5] I might have been better without them. Possibly they intended that I would profit from being in their presence. Perhaps they unwittingly made negative impressions. But the net effect upon me was, I fear, negative. Then, "looking back through the thickening mists," to use Alfred Dennis's macabre phrase, I, too, "see the vivid apparition" of a teacher or two as notable to me as Woodrow Wilson was to Dennis during his Princeton days.[6] In those blessed, providential timings, the right teachers came along and disturbed the stagnant water of my uninspired life. Communicating a fundamental faith in my worth and promise, they moved me out from the small, meager surroundings, upward to larger levels and more prosperous plateaus of aspiration. Often in less overt and obvious ways, they encouraged, challenged, and taught me that I could accomplish and achieve in life. Of such ones I, too, can say a teacher affects eternity.[7]

If an American child could become an elementary school dropout, I would have been it. Elementary school was not one of my favorite places. Of course, I had some good days and some good teachers, but both came infrequently. The cute, nicely dressed, ultrapolite little girls, wearing shiny leather shoes got all the attention and most of the privileges. The well-behaved boys with slicked-back hair and middle-class manners always sat in the front of the class. But the kids from the other side of town—the other side of the tracks—(like me) were never teacher's pet; we got pushed to the periphery. We wore clean but not fashionable clothes. Our hair always needed cutting (when long hair was *not* fashionable). Our parents, who worked in factories, had never finished school. It was tough in those days to climb the educational ladder, and everytime we tried, our weight bore down on weak rungs.

My schoolwork was generally satisfactory, and I received the customary "does his best" on report cards, but the category quaintly labeled *deportment* frequently had checkmarks, indicating lacks in self-discipline, cooperation, manners, and so on. Some categories sounded strange to me. How could I excel in *sociability,* when I didn't even know what the word meant? Although I did satisfactorily, I still dreaded that end-of-the-year report card and promotion day. Trembling, I contemplated the prospect of spending another year back in that grade, with *that* teacher, but my fears always proved unwarranted. Each year I got promoted, or as we said to one another, with wild ecstasy, "I passed!"

Though I must have occasionally felt success in those days, nothing stands out in my mind. Then along came sixth grade and with it, God be praised, my big break! The annual back-to-school-night program for parents turned things around. Each class, from first to sixth, staged its own spectacular. Younger children usually sang a song or recited in unison. Our sixth-grade class put on a skit. For some unexplainable reason, the teacher assigned me a key role. I recited a lengthy poem—a humorous poem—a hilariously humorous poem. Perhaps she had typecast me. Even at that stage, I had developed a not undeserved reputation as the class clown. I could make the class laugh at the drop of the hat. I had carefully cultivated the fine art of witticism. I had a knack for punning, and I could make a joke about the most unlikely event.

When the memorable evening came, the whole school was abuzz. Parents, sitting in stiff wooden seats, waved to their children. Backstage, teachers kept a tight rein on the children who seemed almost unable to contain themselves, like racehorses in their stalls, waiting to explode down the track at the sound of the starting gun. Finally, my moment came. I was in my element. I still recall the audience's reaction. The timing was masterful (I say modestly). Vocal inflections—flawless. The punchlines were delivered precisely. The ovation still rings in my ears. On the report card for that marking period, my teacher noted: "We were pleased with your son's performance at parents' night. It was a stellar accomplishment." I didn't know what *stellar* meant, but found its meaning in the dictionary; from that day, I entertained thoughts of show business. I became a teacher instead—teaching is kind of like show business!

As I look back, I see I used wit and humor as defense mechanisms. Lacking any obvious natural talent and all the social amenities, I felt vulnerable in an every-man-for-himself world. In self-defense, I honed my only weapon to a razor-sharp edge: I was never at a loss for the quick retort. Throughout school, I kept this mark of distinction, and for the high-school yearbook, I was voted most humorous boy in the class. (Ironically, I and the girl voted most humorous both became teachers and both obtained doctorates. In academia, acerbic wit often comes in handy.)

A Critical Impact

I wonder if my influence upon students has equaled the providential and productive one my sixth-grade teacher had on me. What a frightening prospect for affecting eternity and what potential for influencing students! I hope I have not limited my instruction to the perfunctories—those day-to-day requirements, quite essential, but in themselves not too edifying. If a teacher makes no impact upon the critical areas of life—upon desires and values and goals (especially for God's glory)—then all else loses its nobility.

I take comfort (but not complacency) from the few who have graciously acknowledged the little part I have played in their lives. From public-school teaching days, one perennial Christmas card still comes from California, keeping me up-to-date with the news and expressing appreciation, even now, after over two decades. More frequent and more immediate are student contacts from college years of teaching. Many of these people have become fast friends. Their lives have enriched mine, I suspect, more than mine did theirs. Recently a graduating senior, one of my advisees and students, slipped this letter under my office door at the close of the school year:

> This is not your typical letter of gratitude for the learning and growth you've fostered within this apprentice. Nor is it meant to be a graduating senior's thank-you for all the good times and fond memories. That isn't to say I'm not grateful. (I am more than you know.) But I think you'd probably respond with something humble like, "I'm just doing my job."
>
> It's quite true that much of my time spent in your classroom and as your advisee has nurtured me both as a student and as a fellow Christian. However, I would hope that this letter, this note . . . could be a gift of encouragement to you. I assume by now you're wondering what college has done to this poor girl's head. Well, it's done a lot. And thanks to God's infinite grace, what it's done has been at least 90 percent good. I wonder if you, as a professor, actually get to observe the changes that go on in the transformation of a freshman to a senior. . . . Perhaps I am attempting to say thank-you, and I suppose this letter will end up another piece of senior sentimental garb. But I honestly believe it goes further than emotionalism. Because of your willingness . . . one of your students . . . has become stronger and maybe even a bit wiser person.

There have been other letters and notes—most of them kind and undeservedly complimentary. I kept some for a while, but fearing I might linger complacently with those numbing affirmations, eventually I burned them. The sentiments, however, sweetly aromatic, remain within my breathing space.

In college teaching, the transformation from freshman to senior is a startling one. Students enter college with pubescent exuberance and extravagant energy; gradually, maturity molds the mind and shapes the spirit. I marvel at their metamorphosis. One freshman I recall seemed the most hopeless prospect I had ever encountered. His ill-fitting clothes, boorish manner, and immaturity marked him as an unpromising candidate for college work, but he wanted to become a teacher. Early experiences with him in class did nothing to change my initial impression, but he did try hard. Although I gave him little chance of success, I admired his determination. Gradually I realized that he had a certain unaffected charm. He made no attempts at pretense and was open—wide open—to guidance. Eagerly taking in things, slowly he began to change—barely discernible bits of change at first, but slowly my student shed the gloomy cocoon of awkwardness. He became less impulsive and more reflective, without diminishing his eagerness to learn. Although he made it through the academic program and gained some competence and a degree of social skill, his rustic, backwoods style remained evident at graduation. I wrote several cautious recommendations for him, uncertain of what lay ahead. However, when he returned to campus several years later, I beheld an almost unbelievable transformation. Impeccably attired, articulate, almost debonair, he told about his success as a teacher. He had received outstanding evaluations, and now he was undertaking graduate studies at the university. He talked appreciatively of the years he spent at college and thanked me for my small part in them. After completing a graduate degree, he attended seminary, intending to become a seminary professor. Perhaps my glimmer of hope for this young man when he first arrived at college was similar to the one my college professors had had for me decades before.

The Mystical Membership

Teaching is a God-ordained task. Christ gave the gift of teachers to His church (Ephesians 4:11). Especially for small children, who see them as phantoms, materializing only between the hours of schooltime, teachers have always had a certain aura. As part of a favored fraternity, belonging to a mystical membership, even though others may not always appreciate them, teachers forge character in young lives. Christa McAuliffe, the lone teacher aboard the ill-fated *Challenger* shuttle, recognized this when she said: "I touch the future; I teach."

A select group of teachers have achieved a degree of fame and received some tributes from their students.[8] Peter Drucker, economist, author, and successful teacher himself, takes a full chapter in a book devoted to "people . . . worth recording, worth thinking about" to talk about two fourth-grade teachers who "were not just good, they were outstanding."[9] No accolades given any teacher are more memorable than those with which Helen Keller extols her own teacher: "I learned a great many new words that day. I do not remember what they all were; but I do know that . . . teacher [was] among them . . . to make the world blossom for me."[10]

Countless other teachers, unheralded and unknown beyond their community, have also given themselves unsparingly, with meager reward for their service. Hidden away in classrooms, in less than comfortable or commodious settings, persisting in the tedium that the task of teaching can often become, they have transformed lives by precept and example.

In the educational community, a fledgling teacher can try his wings and perhaps soar into the rarefied atmosphere of excellence, but not without facing perils. To assume the mantle of teacher means wrapping oneself in other people's lives. No educator can afford the luxury of aloofness. Within the citadel of a student's soul are held the aspirations of eternity. In the confrontation between teacher and student exists the possibility of cosmic grandeur. The student can grow, develop, explore, and actualize or be forced into the small shell of an aborted life. As teacher and student engage each other on the sharp, piercing edge of destiny, neither will return from the meeting quite the same. Changes occur. Transformations take place. Each comes away with part of the other and leaves part of himself there. Teaching involves anguish, because investment in lives requires the sacrifice of part of one's soul.

The Challenge to Students

Notable thinkers and writers whose works have been called masterpieces declare their indebtedness to teachers. John Stuart Mill, tutored by his father and given instruction in Greek at the age of three, says his father "exerted an amount of labor, care and perseverance rarely, if ever employed for a similar purpose in endeavoring to give . . . the highest . . . education."[11] The intellectually precocious Mill claimed his father's instruction placed him at least a quarter of a century ahead of his contemporaries. He attributed his capacity for logical reasoning and skill in the analysis of argumentation to the daily efforts of his father.

> . . .He first attempted by questions to make me think on the subject, and frame some conception of what constituted the utility of syllogistic logic. . . . My own consciousness and experience ultimately led me to appreciate as highly as he did the value of early practical familiarity with school logic. I know of nothing in my education, to which I think myself more indebted for whatever capacity for thinking I have attained.[12]

C. S. Lewis, poet, polemicist, and Christian apologist, achieved a rare reconciliation between the imaginative and the rational—literary creativity and cerebral logic. He wrote whimsical fantasy like the Narnia tales and penned his space trilogy in science-fiction genre. But Lewis also wrote prose with a logical precision that prompted Clyde Kilby of Wheaton College, in Illinois, a Lewis scholar, to remark that Lewis possessed a "remarkable combination of two qualities normally supposed to be opposites. I mean on the one hand a deep vivid imagination and on the other a profound analytic mind."[13]

Before becoming a student at Oxford, Lewis sat in tutorials with W. T. Kirkpatrick, whom he described as being the closest thing to "a purely logical entity." Kirkpatrick's incisive and relentless questioning and insistence upon irrefutable logic branded itself upon Lewis's method of inquiry and surfaced in his writing style. Lewis's "cold blooded reason" was acquired from Kirkpatrick and "to a boy steeped in the joys of reading, Kirkpatrick's house was a paradise."[14]

Education is not a matter of spontaneous generation. Educational life comes from teachers who live. Teachers disseminate. Teachers seminate! They plant seeds and cultivate them in a climate of caring—a kindergarten of a kind where "kinder-caring" will nurture new life and growth within learners. As nurturers teachers attend to growth and provide conditions conducive to development. Each broods expectantly, alert to the moments of teachableness, those optimum learning times. Sylvia Ashton-Warner, who spent years teaching the Maori people, tells of this process in her journal:

> "They became part of me. . . . And what is the birth? A long, perpetuating, never-ending, transmuting birth, beginning its labor every morning and a rest between pains every evening."[15]

A Call to Growth

Christian teachers, particularly, must view their task as a calling. Summoned by the One who has given them the life-changing challenge of educating lives, Christian teachers respond to His invitation as a stewardship—a sacred trust. Faithful in the performance of these privileged tasks, disciplined by the constraining love of Christ, Christian teachers become neither demagogues nor despots. They must take their students by the hand and lead them, purposefully yet gently, through the curriculum of godly grace. The route and circuit they travel covers the *paideia* (discipline) of God's direction. Challenges, strategically designed and deployed to bring out the best student effort, provide occasions for progress. Discerning teachers maintain this deliberate and delicate balance between the pull of gentle persuasion and the push of spirited prodding.

At the same time the Christian teacher must always aim at full growth—maturity in Christ—which requires carefulness and precision. A headlong, impetuous rush toward completion leads to premature, inchoate forms that cannot survive in a world that takes its toll on the ill-prepared. As Christian teachers commit themselves to this responsibility, their lives become ministries in nurturing. Their goals become the ones envisioned by American educator Francis Parker: "If I should tell you the secret of my life, it is the intense desire that I have to see growth and development in human beings. I think that the whole secret of my enthusiasm and study, if there be any secret to it—my intense desire to see mind and soul grow."[16]

We may simply define teaching as the growth in soul and mind. Much of what passes for education in some academic circles is regressive and mis-educative, as Paul Goodman has polemically put it.[17] However, Christian teachers operate from a biblical mandate that sends them in search of ever-expanding and efficacious ways to have students grow in grace, knowledge, and godliness (2 Peter 3:18) If only we can find one teacher who is for us and who offers achievable challenges, we can be freed from the provincialism of narrow and gnarled worlds! With continued amazement and gratefulness, I recall those gentle influences on my own life.

During the war-weary years, with their ubiquitous blackouts and CLOSED FOR DURATION signs, I found one place of solace in the local library. There an unpretentious, little, white-haired teacher who had an after-school "reading time corner" every Friday taught me the value and virtue of books. For one hour she read to whoever attended. Often I would be the only person there, but she read anyhow. Her lilting voice and dramatic gestures made the stories live. After story hour, I gathered my armful of library books and marched home, consumed in reading for the weekend. She instilled in me the love for words and intrigued me with the charm of stories. Though society was marred by deprivation, I could always escape between the covers of a borrowed book, into adventure and enchantment. Even now, when with the luxury of leisure I browse through libraries, the face of that unforgotten teacher smiles on me with encouragement and affirmation.

As I moved along through school, a few other teachers penetrated the deceptively unpromising exterior of a dull schoolboy. They commented favorably on an exceptionally well-written paper or greeted unexpected, insightful answers to puzzling questions with restrained approval. They kept my momentum going.

In high school, Miss Hogan, tall and lean, with a wry sense of humor, prodded me into thinking about new possibilities. She invited me to dinner on all occasions (unheard of in those days), probed my thinking on a number of contemporary issues, and applauded my responses. I was chosen for the four-member quiz team that competed against other area high schools. The competitions aired on radio. She coached and coaxed the team. Under her relentless but caring mentoring, we achieved a runner-up position in the final competition—something never before done (or accomplished since) in the history of that school. With fondness, I reflect on the inspiration she provided. Endless hours she spent—her only reward was the satisfaction of having her team succeed. With firmness and fairness, she goaded us toward a sometimes seemingly impossible goal. She taught me to extend my reach. Miss Hogan was a teacher of reachers! She never settled for anything less than the best we had, but would always make us content with that.

But among all those who taught me, no one stands out so singularly as Mitch, who held no degrees. He had attended no college, nor had he completed high school. His only classrooms were the Sunday-morning circle of young boys and the streets and alleyways of their lives. His influence was not limited to Sundays, nor did it stop at the front door of the church. Controlled casualness and firm devotion to Christ's leading characterized his style, and he defined his task in terms of eternity.

Week after week and all the days in between, he entered our lives, always bringing the Savior with him. His lessons in the bedrock realities of day-to-day living were sweetened by the grace of the Lord Jesus. "Be sweet," he would say. "Be sweet."

Mitch never pontificated or preached at us. Neither did he intimidate or harangue. Yet he treated his Sunday-school lessons like the serious concerns they were. After a few light moments of talk about sports, school, and the week's events, he took us straight to the Savior—to the Christ he had come to know later in his life. With his facility for bringing the Bible into the everyday, hard-knocks world of a grimy, air-polluted town, he made us breathe the pure air of heaven. Talking about politeness and kindness, he gently encouraged us to show Christian courtesy in a factory town where those things were rare. Like ripples in a pond, his influence on lives spread expansively beyond that group of boys. Those taught by Mitch are now numbered among the preachers and missionaries and businessmen—and teachers, too.

Learning involves growth, and all these teachers encouraged growth. Some planted, some watered, as the apostle Paul reminds us, but in the final analysis, God gives the increase (1 Corinthians 3:6). These teachers had a holy restlessness about them, and they continually grew. They helped us sort out our priorities, sharpen our perspectives, and they shaped in us a clear sense of propriety and proportion. I saw in them the even balance between the temporal and the eternal—that necessary sense of spiritual proportion. Even as the memorable Mr. Chips lamented the lack of the grasp of proportion in some schoolboys, those teachers would not let our lives become unbalanced. ". . . No sense of proportion—that was the matter with them, these new fellows. . . . No sense of proportion. And it was a sense of proportion, above all things . . . to teach."[18]

Never could I repay the debt I owe these teachers, except by allowing the part of them that remains in me to find profitable lodging in others whom I touch. Truly old teachers never die, they simply "lesson" themselves in others.

2

A MODEL STUDENT

Study to show thyself approved unto God, a workman that needeth not to be ashamed. . . .

2 Timothy 2:15

Alas! The genius of our age, from schools
less humble, draws her lessons, aims and rules. . . .[1]

They from their native selves can send abroad
Like transformations, for themselves create
a like existence, and whene're it is
created for them, catch it by an instinct;
. . . they build up greatest things
from least suggestions, ever on the watch,
willing to work and to be wrought upon,
. . . such minds are truly from the Deity.[2]

Probably the most gifted student I had ever encountered in a classroom, Gail excelled at everything. Her reading ability was superior. New words she considered briefly and then read flawlessly. She could derive their meanings from their contexts or from clues within the words themselves. The day following the assassination of President John F. Kennedy, all public schools in our state scheduled a special memorial service. At a hastily assembled program in our school the commemorative article in the *New York Times* was chosen to be read, and Gail was selected to read it, sight unseen. Only in seventh grade, she read it errorlessly, pronouncing every word correctly. On another occasion, when she missed a complete week of school with illness, she submitted a report on the origins of the English language (well in excess of one hundred pages) when she returned. She said she did it for extra credit, because she had so much free time while she was sick.

Where Are the Model Students?

Most students do not act like Gail. The majority are well meaning, reasonably complacent, capable of performing better, and satisfied that their parents and government require them to attend school; but often they see little relationship between what goes on there and "real life." For many, school means the temporary suspension of ambition. A noted lecturer, addressing an audience of college students, stopped abruptly when the undercurrent of disinterested chatter became annoyingly high and said brusquely: "I did not come expecting interest on your part. College, you have no doubt learned, is a place where nothing is expected of you. You have a four year hiatus to be utterly irresponsible without having to suffer any dire consequences. I did, however, perhaps naively, expect a modicum of respect.''

Over the years many schools have not developed a too favorable reputation. For numbers of students, the whimsical reminiscences of schooldays by James Whitcomb Riley are more fancy than fact:

> *Midst the wealth of fact and fancy*
> *that our memories may recall*
> *thus the old school-day romances*
> *are the dearest, after all.*[3]

For generations of disenchanted students, more often the memories resemble James Jordan's cynical characterization: ''Many so-called colleges and universities are ghoul-havens harboring ''Teachers'' whose sole (soul?) activity consists of pruning and dwarfing the minds of those misfortunates called students—much in the fashion of Japanese bonsai tree masters.''[4]

If the accounts of school life popularized by some great storytellers are half true, students see schools as grim places indeed. Many have read of wretched Master Squeers of Dotheboys Hall, who delighted ''in disregarding a piteous cry for mercy,'' and eagerly ''fell upon the boy and caned him soundly; not leaving off, indeed, until his arm was tired out.''[5] In *Jane Eyre* Charlotte Brontë makes her readers dislike Lowood School with its ''irksome struggle'' and ''unwonted tasks'' and the constant ''fear of failure'' that harassed Jane constantly.[6] In such situations neither student nor teacher provides a model.

But scattered here and there throughout reflective writings we find occasional tributes to more accommodating schools and to schoolmasters more gently inclined to the task of teaching. The legendary ''Arnold of Rugby,'' popularized in *Tom Brown's School Days,* was one kindly exception to the unflattering stereotype of the teacher: ''But it was this thoroughness and undaunted courage which more than anything else won his way to the hearts . . . and made them believe first in him and then in his

Master.''[7] Such a man must have attracted his fair share of model students.

What of Jesus, the tender teacher who never once lifted a hand to thrash a student (only wretched money changers)? If anyone deserved model students, the Son of God did. Yet a quick look shows that the twelve seemed far from the best models, by human standards. Jesus rebuked the disciples when they obstructed the path of children whose mothers brought them to Him; then He took the children in His arms and gave His paternal and pedagogical blessing (Mark 10:13–16).

Most teachers who knew as much of their students as Jesus knew of His twelve would have gone out of their way to avoid the fiery-tempered ''sons of thunder'' or the volatile fisherman Peter. How many would have spent any time at all upon the unsavory Judas? Though the disciples hardly seemed the most suitable candidates for schooling, Jesus willingly invested time and energy (education is always costly). He sought the best in them and they did not disappoint Him in the end.

Reachable and Teachable

Before a teacher can do anything with a student, he or she must be close at hand—reachable. After Christ had attracted the disciples to Himself, He took them home. ''Where do you live?'' they asked. ''Come and see,'' He replied (John 1:38, 39).

I have had numerous students to my home through the years; there they see me in a more human place. It is more difficult to ''fake it'' when students experience your family life and see you interact with your wife and children. The bell doesn't sound, ending the session. At home you find it harder to hide behind the teacher role. Students see how you furnish your house and the kind of meals you eat. They hear your wife call you by your first name (or perhaps she uses quaint, affectionate terms). Occasionally, I watch the reaction of students caught off guard by their teacher being called ''honey.'' He spills gravy on his shirt. He even helps clear the dinner table. Revelations!

I've gone to students' houses as well. A while back, I developed a fond and friendly relationship with parents of one student. The couple had married young, were not much older than I, and had a charming daughter. I shared their meals on several occasions. A few years after the daughter left my class, her father died unexpectedly. Because we had touched each other's worlds, I shared in their sorrow, and I still hear from her from time to time.

Amenable is the euphemism we used on the most receptive students' cumulative records. Teachers never want to say outright that the student is blessedly easy to teach. Instead, we used educationese—"amenable to learning." Model students have a bent—a proclivity—for learning. They are *eager* to learn; for them, school holds the wonder of discovery. As I saw the library in my youth, they see the school building beckoning with the generosity of growth. "Come find yourself here," it seems to say. "This is where you belong. We were made for each other."

George Sheehan, cardiac specialist and marathon runner, reports an incident that occurred in the kindergarten class where his daughter taught. Customarily one of the children offered a little prayer at cookies-and-milk time. As Sheehan tells it: "Last week, a pupil who had been a constant joy to her took his opportunity and exclaimed, 'Thank you, God, for school!' Eureka! The great discovery that God and school go together. That school was a place for joy—for delight—dare we say, for ecstasy. Somewhere an astounded creator clapped His hands. One of His creatures had understood His creation."[8]

Caught, then taught! That's the sequence of education. Captivated and liberated! The paradoxical alignment. The apostle Paul, wise in the ways of ancient pedagogy, recruited his students in similar fashion. Their affection for him followed their attraction to him (chapter 16 of Romans supports this assertion). Attraction then education. Socrates' famous pupil, Plato, uses his mentor as his spokesman in all his dialogues. Socrates' style of questioning for truth attracted the young man. Plato in turn transmitted this style to his pupil Aristotle, who established the basis for Western intellectual thought. Aristotle entered Plato's Academy at the age of seventeen and remained until he was forty. Good pupils form an affiliation with good teachers.

Meekness is the agreeable prerequisite for the model student. Like a horse that has been broken, model students obediently channel their energies toward the teacher's direction and resist dissipating their strength through unruly impetuosity. Haughty "unbroken" necks cannot wear yokes that harness model students to their schoolmasters and allow learning to take place. Two tread the same educational terrain when they agree (Matthew 11:29). The apostle Paul was a model student. However, as Saul of Tarsus, headstrong and arrogant, defiantly disregarding the goads against which he kicked like a bucking bronco, Jesus confronted him on the Damascus road and "broke him." (Acts 9:1–6). Saul spent the next three years in a wilderness tutorial, meekly learning the revelations he would share with the churches (Galatians 1:15–18).

They have sat in my classes. Arms crossed. Faces frowning. The nonverbal message plain: *I dare you to teach me anything*! For the most part, I haven't. There can be no spark, no ignition, when the poles are apart, and we *were* apart. I could cajole, coerce, threaten if I wanted, but my blandishments met with granite resistance. An immovable object: But my force was not irresistible.

But others, pliably attentive, invited instruction as the pistil on the flower waits for the pollen to drop. Leo Buscaglia describes the meek student as one with "kind eyeballs." By that, he means a radiant receptivity to teaching. The sparkle in the eye signals a sensitivity in the heart. Whenever Buscaglia talks to audiences or teaches his classes (most of them large), he searches for these "eyeballs." If he fails to find them, he knows nothing will happen in that class.

Undeniably, self-discipline ranks near the top in the hierarchy of the marks of the model-student. Indulgence, which makes caprice the basis for all decisions, will soon spend the treasures the mind has stored. Diligence determines the profit of education. *Discipline* has fallen into disrepute in education; students say it smacks of regimentation and thwarts creativity. Of course, they define *creativity* as spontaneity in the rawest sense. Impulse alone dictates and decrees action. But students need restrictions and have to learn the major lesson of becoming their own masters in this vital area. Until we establish parameters, worthwhile accomplishments cannot occur. Before the game can begin, we need to agree on ground rules. Discipline demands the drudgery of hard work. Forgoing legitimate pleasures for future prospects is imperative and inescapable. How quickly the time has passed since my college days (three decades ago), when I found it hard to resist the temptation to call it quits. Like many students of that generation, I worked my way through school on the graveyard shift (midnight to eight). With limited funds, too few hours of sleep, and the incessant demands of a difficult college program, I battled the daily allurement of dropping out into something less immediately demanding. But by God's grace, strength surfaced during my periods of desperate weakness (2 Corinthians 12:9), and commencement came none too soon. Idle hours spent in early stages yield nothing but barrenness at later times. Learning is *hard* work.

Several years ago, a student came to my office, complaining about his poor school performance. It didn't take long to determine his problem: He lacked discipline. The solution was less easy than the diagnosis. He had developed a pattern of irresponsibility throughout the semester.

"What'll I do?" he asked imploringly. "I'll fail for sure, the way I'm going."

I commended him for his keen insight.

"Can you help me?" he pleaded.

"I can *help*, but I can't *solve* your problem," I answered candidly. "What you need is some organization and order in your life. If you want to continue college, then clearly you will have to focus more sharply and behave accordingly. In other words, you need discipline." His silence told me the word was foreign to his academic vocabulary. "Let's work on some sort of schedule for your time and activity," I suggested. "Let's block out the time during the week when you're committed to something— class, study, work, sleep, whatever. Then we'll make some decisions about how the unscheduled time is to be spent. Understand?'' He nodded compliantly.

We spent the next hour arranging a schedule that accounted for all his time during the week. After we finished, I said, ''Sign it.'' He looked quizzical. ''Sign it,'' I repeated. ''I want your word that you'll do what you say you'll do. The only way you'll get your life turned around is to assume responsibility for it and discipline yourself.'' He signed his name. ''Now come back in a week,'' I ordered, ''but only if you've kept to the schedule. It's a week's trial. If it doesn't work out, then there's little I can do, so we don't want to waste each other's time, do we?'' He nodded.

One week later, he returned. ''I did it!'' he exclaimed proudly. ''Good,'' I answered. ''Now do it again this next week.''

Soon he was back on course. I saw him infrequently after that. He finished the year satisfactorily and eventually graduated. A happy ending!

By discipline, I do not mean a forced, unnatural regimentation that circumscribes every behavior and imposes unreasonable limitations. Discipline is the recognition of legitimate consequences and the willingness, in the light of those consequences, to choose a course of behavior that will maximize benefits in terms of wisely chosen goals. Invariably and unmistakably that involves self-denial. Whether by denial of the use of time or other resources, the tough choices that refuse the little luxuries of the present for the great prospects of the future will characterize the disciplined student's life. Likewise all great artists testify to the long hours of privation they have accepted to reach their goals.

During my doctoral program, I observed that the basic difference between students who completed the degree and those who did not was the willingness to forego the little luxuries. The ABD is not uncommon in higher education—''*all but dissertation.*'' After all courses have been taken, the simple but painful commitment to the dissertation separates the PhD from the ABD. I know students who have long since completed their course work, but the doctorate still eludes them, because they have never finished the thesis. As a graduate advisor once told his doctoral candidate: "If you don't have the dissertation, you don't have nuttin'."

If I may be permitted a temporary lapse of modesty, I can point to my own children as examples of teachableness and discipline. During their school careers, they consistently devoted themselves to learning. Schools were joyful places for them. Teachers, for the most part, encouraged and motivated. They took their school assignments seriously and typically went the extra mile, becoming actively involved in all phases of the school program. My older daughter maintained outstanding academic standards while engaging in band and orchestra, competing on speech teams, editing the yearbook, and taking part in a host of other activities. My younger daughter excelled in music, diligently practicing and participating in numerous events. They committed themselves to daily practice and study; they resisted the allure of extraneous enticements; and they pursued goals that awaited future fulfillment. My son, who never lived to graduate from the school he loved was *the* model student. Meek and amenable, an inner determination for excellence consistently controlled him. Disciplined beyond his years, he never lapsed into irresponsibility or indifference. School and he were made for each other. He got out of bed each day without prodding from his parents, completed assignments punctually, and kept his books in order. He was an honor student and found creative outlets in a variety of areas, but he especially loved the trumpet and practiced it diligently. He set personal goals and, spurred on by an inner drive, devoted uncounted hours to achieving excellence.

The Vision of Curiosity

Beyond the discipline, however, the model student feels a sense of curiosity and wonder. He opens himself to experiences, and like King David, the extraordinarily talented son of Jesse, embraces a wide range of interests. Abraham Maslow, noted psychologist, identifies "openness to experience" as a mark of the self-actualized student.[9] The disciples who surrounded the Lord were willing to be taken through the trauma of new adventure. Complacency that never tests itself will never know the wonder of learning, for learning requires liberty to move beyond small borders and boundaries that keep us from "green pastures."

For more than a decade, I have sponsored a college cross-culture study tour, taking hundreds of students to cities, towns, and hidden-away hamlets in Greece, Turkey, other countries in Eastern Europe, and to some less frequently traveled spots of the world. They have the opportunity, for a short time, to live a life so unlike their too comfortably familiar ones; they experience the maniacal pace of modern Athens, the lazy flow of life in obscure villages in mountainous Crete, the oriental bazaars of Istanbul. They move beyond their usual limits, and they grow. John Dewey would approve of our efforts: "But liberty for the child is the chance to test all impulses and tendencies on the world of things and people in which he finds himself sufficiently to discover their character so that he may get rid of those things which are harmful and develop those things which are useful to himself and others."[10]

Poet Robert Browning, at the age of seventy-five, wrote a poem about the encouragement his father gave him when he showed interest in Homer's writings. As his father read the *Iliad* Browning asked curiously what he read. His father replied: "The siege of Troy." "What's a *siege*?" the boy inquired. Unlike those who may dismiss such subjects as too difficult for children, Browning's father boosted the boy's curiosity by proceeding to build an imaginary city from the tables and chairs and explained the *Iliad*. At eight years old, Robert Browning began reading the *Iliad*, and his father encouraged him to read it in Greek.[11]

Jesus never stifled curiosity. He would not, of course, cater to the unreasonable requests of the Pharisees or Herod. But when the disciples saw Christ praying and requested that He teach them to pray, He gave them the "model prayer" (Luke 11:1–4). When asked if He would restore the kingdom, Jesus outlined the design of the ages in the Olivet discourse (Matthew 24:3–25:46). Any evidence of sincere inquiry would prompt a detailed lesson from the Master.

The "whys" and "what ifs" have been catalysts for many fresh discoveries. Alexander Graham Bell, seeking a way to help his hearing-impaired wife, invented the telephone. Peter Goldmark, dissatisfied with the disruption of changing phonograph records, invented the long-play record. Challenged to develop some product that customers could use, dispose of, and purchase again, King Gillette stumbled upon the idea of the disposable razor, while shaving one morning.

One of the most *un*inspired classes I ever taught was a first-period (8:00 A.M.) American history class of blasé, self-satisfied, supercilious, but quite capable and academically keen high-school seniors. They were in a state of educational *ennui*—flaccid, bored, disinterested, and absolutely *un*curious. On the other hand, one of my most exhilarating teaching experiences involved the class that followed that soporific schoolday start—a "catch-all" class in problems of democracy (a euphemism for "try to teach them anything"). Seniors bursting with energy! Uninhibited and spontaneous, the class blazed with questions, and the subject slithered like a snake, taking whatever sinuous form the students wanted. The first period sat stagnantly interested only in the security of their inflated grade-point average. They envisioned college as the upward-mobility start toward success and assurance of a place in the Great American Dream. The second-period students scratched and clawed to hang in until graduation. Several of the girls were pregnant and would settle prematurely into the dull routine of soap operas and shopping. The boys seemed dismally preoccupied with the draft, during this era of the Vietnam War. But for one year, at least, they had a zest for living. Sometimes my nerves frayed, trying to cope with their exuberance, which, cyclonelike, threatened to sweep through the room. The year's curriculum reduced itself to two major topics for them: sex and religion. Irrespective of the assignment, eventually the class discussion made its way around to one of these issues. Students actually moved from the rear of the room to the front of the class on their own initiative—the holy grail of teaching! Their ears perked up at these topics. What the two had in common, of course, was *life*—propagation of human life and the prospect (or lack) of eternal life. Without violating the legal restrictions, I let the topics take us where they would. One rare but highly treasured memento from those schooldays remains with me. The second period presented me with an onyx desk set with the simple inscription "FROM YOUR SECOND-PERIOD CLASS."

Wholesight Vision

Model students must combine what Parker Palmer calls "the eye of the mind" with "the eye of the heart" into "wholesight vision."[12] Approval must come not only from men, but from God. Vision means more than seeing; it requires sight and *in*-sight. At some juncture in the learning, heaven and earth must intersect. Education requires spiritual interpretation. One-sighted vision, like that of the Cyclops of Greek mythology, can serve only to build walls, and that sight will darken when the mind's eye alone sees. Pascal, the French philosopher, understood the need for vision from within and confessed that "the heart has reasons that reason knows not of."

The apostle Peter became a two-sighted student of Christ. Paul needed to be blinded to let the vision of his heart open. All students of the Savior must likewise fuse the focus of head and heart. "If . . . thine eye be single," Jesus said, "thy whole body shall be full of light." (Matthew 6:22). Paul prayed that the "eyes of your heart may be opened" (*see* Ephesians 1:18).

Helen Keller identified the most important day of her life when her teacher, Anne Sullivan, came to her. Although sightless, Helen undertook, with the gentle guidance of her teacher, an education that gave her a view of life few sighted people have shared. Like a ship at sea, engulfed in dense fog, Helen groped, crying out for help: "Light! Give me light! was the wordless cry of my soul and the light of love shone on me in that very hour."

Helen Keller progressed in her learning, and one day she asked her teacher the meaning of the word *love*. She had brought some flowers to her teacher, and her teacher tried to kiss her, but Helen resisted this expression of affection. "I love Helen," her teacher told her.

"What is love?" I asked.

She drew me closer to her and said, "it is here," pointing to my heart whose beats I was conscious of for the first time. Her words puzzled me very much because I did not then understand anything unless I touched it. I smelt the violets in her hand and asked, half in words, half in signs, a question which meant, "Is love the sweetness of flowers?"

"No," said my teacher.

Again I thought. The warm sun was shining on us. "Is this not love?" I asked, pointing in the direction from which the heat came, "Is this not love?"

It seemed to me that there could be nothing more beautiful than the sun, whose warmth makes all things grow. But Miss Sullivan shook her head and I was greatly puzzled and disappointed. I thought it strange that my teacher could not show me love. . . .

Again I asked my teacher, "Is this not love?"

"Love is something like the clouds that were in the sky before the sun came out," she replied. ". . . You cannot touch the clouds, you know; but you feel the rain and know how glad the flowers and the thirsty earth are to have it after a hot day. You cannot touch love either; but you feel the sweetness that it pours into everything. Without love you would not be happy or want to play."

The beautiful truth burst upon my mind—I felt that there were invisible lines stretched between my spirit and the spirit of others.[13]

The model student learns that lines stretch between God's Spirit and his spirit, and those lines then stretch from him to others.

3

THE WONDER
OF THE WORD

Thy word is a lamp unto my feet, and a light unto my path.

Psalms 119:105

Spiritual discernment and ordinary intelligence are needed in the study of Holy Scripture. Spirituality is the prime essential, for the spiritual truths are spiritually discerned; but common sense, to use the popular phrase, will generally save us from the follies of false exegesis.[1]

He moved among all human contact with unerring grace. . . . He always suited his strength to our weakness. . . . He was a man of the rarest and most delicate breeding, the first and truest gentleman we had known. Had he been nothing else, how much we would have learnt from that alone.[2]

B efore education can take place, you must have a teacher (one who has some expertise) and a student (one who wishes to learn). For the Christian, this has also involved the study of the Bible and growth in Christlikeness. Indeed, those who believe in Him often see education from a different viewpoint than that of the non-Christian.

From the beginning, some Americans have closely connected the importance of literacy and God's Word, and early American education owed much to the importance colonists placed upon literacy. In 1642 and 1647 Massachusetts Bay Colony passed two important laws, mandating "the ability to read and understand the principles of religion." The second law, known as the "Old Deluder Satan Act," prescribed schoolmasters and schools for towns large enough to accommodate them. Undeniably, they saw that the Bible formed the basis for the need for literacy so that the deluder, Satan, could not "keep men from the knowledge of the Scriptures." The leading historian of American education documents the primacy of the Bible in the educational life of the colonists: "The Bible was read and recited, quoted and consulted, early committed to memory and constantly searched for meaning. Deemed universally relevant it remained throughout the century the single most important cultural influence in the lives of Anglo-Americans. . . . And so men turned to the Bible with reverence and restless curiosity. . . ."[3]

In a recent interview on national television, an illiterate woman, asked why she wanted to learn to read, tearfully replied, "So I can read the Bible." The Christian religion, someone has said, is the religion of the *Book*! Wherever the Bible has gone throughout the world, literacy has followed. The extensive efforts in translating the Scriptures into many languages testify to the importance of the Bible in life and its impact on promoting literacy.

My own love for God's Word began in Sunday-school classes, with faithful teachers, when still the innocence of godly things was with me. My comprehension of the Word and recognition of its eternal worth came more forcibly during the Daily Vacation Bible School days, in those years when we youngsters had little to do in the summer but roam the streets or swim in the yet unpolluted streams. At first I did not attend out of fascination or interest. The prodding of the pastor and the persistence of teachers in that Bible Presbyterian Church translated into a concern for my soul I could not easily disregard or dismiss. Wisely, that church ran the Vacation Bible School program immediately after the public-school term ended, leaving us no time to decide to seek other pastimes. (I learned years later that my church pioneered DVBS). Although the day's program included playful activities, basically, the school was a *school*, where the Bible *alone* was taught (along with a catechism). The *five*-week, four-hour daily program rigorously emphasized Bible memorization, recitation, reading, and listening to Bible stories.

Because our leaders provided incentives for daily and weekly attendance as well as a picnic at the end, for everyone who had not missed a day, absenteeism was rare. In a community offering lamentably few rewards, the books given for memorization, the daily ration of candy, and the grand inducement of an all-day picnic (with all the hot dogs you could eat) gave more incentive than anyone needed.

Much of the Scripture I still recall was learned "by heart" in *that* Bible school. There we each committed to memory many Psalms, lengthy portions of the Old Testament (including the Ten Commandments—verbatim), and the Beatitudes, along with portions of the Epistles. And they had to be recited flawlessly! At the conclusion of the five-week term, during an awards evening, the students demonstrated what they had learned and received recognition for their accomplishments. The school was structured like the public school, with grades for each year and several classes for each grade. A specified amount of work constituted the curriculum for each grade. If students completed that work within the five-week period, they could review the previous year's work and gain credit by reciting what they recalled. At the awards ceremony, ribbons were given for satisfactory completion of the curriculum—red ribbons for regular class work and blue ribbons for review work. Greek contestants in the ancient Olympic games could not have considered their laurel victory wreaths greater prizes than I considered those cherished ribbons. I clutched them with great pride.

In that school the Bible was taught patiently and systematically. Students learned their way through its pages and stories. Our fingers quickly found obscure passages, and our tongues recited lengthy portions without error. The King James Version alone was used back then, and I still treasure its contents and elegance. I learned to love the poetry in its pages. Although I now use many translations for personal study, my affection for the Authorized Version has not diminished.

The Word of Truth

We can approach Scripture from a variety of ways. Like nuggets of gold, its truth can be mined by our diligent probing; like grapes full and ripe on ready vines, we may glean its goodness. Never may we exhaust the Bible's wealth, and the spiritual treasures it contains are incapable of depletion. However, we can tap into Scripture at different levels, to extract core samples that provide fresh understanding of strata of God's truth; or we can rediscover spiritual terrain over which others have already trod. One of the special ways of approaching Scripture is from the point of view of *pedagogy*. The Word of God is not *simply* a textbook of ethics and morals, but it is in its enormity, both a primer and a full prospectus for growth in the Christian life. From the fountainhead of God's Word, we drink instruction. There He has written things for our learning (1 Corinthians 10:11; 2 Timothy 3:16).

Guide for Godliness

By pronouncement, precept, and practice, God taught His Old Testament people. The Torah was the book of instruction, and the prophet was God's principal teacher. Within the family, the father assumed the responsibility for instruction in righteousness (Deuteronomy 6:7). When the synagogue emerged (during the Babylonian captivity), instruction became, additionally, an institutional function; learned scribes and rabbis tutored God's people. Then the New Testament light dawns, and the Lord Jesus Christ comes with authority to prescribe and explicate a new teaching, which never contradicts the old, but complements, clarifies, and completes it. His teaching is not His own, for He declares that the Father who sent Him is its source (John 7:16). As the Sent One from heaven, Christ instructs the people He has come to redeem. The grace of God that brings salvation teaches us as well (Titus 2:11–14).

The Teacher of teachers comes with "grace and truth," and His words command attention. Spoken not for the scholar's analysis but for the student's application, "gracious words . . . proceeded out of his mouth" (Luke 4:22). Throughout the Old Testament, God had provided, in shadow and simile, a textbook and guide into godliness. Rich in variety and symbolism, before the full dawning of the revelation in Christ Jesus, the divine record disclosed God's dealings with His people. The approach was ". . . precept upon precept; line upon line, line upon line; here a little, and there a little" (Isaiah 28:10).

The Old Testament "types" that foreshadow the coming Christ are richly expressive. With the British barrister's clarity Sir Robert Anderson elucidates the doctrine of the types in his writings and takes this generation to task for its neglect of the treasure in the typological significance of Old Testament teaching.[4] The writer of the Epistle to the Hebrews, schooled in Old Testament symbolism, contends that God used these pictures as representations of a far greater reality. God spoke at that time in "sign language." Since Christ's coming, God speaks in "Son language" (*see* Hebrews 1:1, 2)

After the call of Abraham and the commission to Moses, God particularly communicated through varied imagery and veiled speech. Throughout the Pentateuch, step by step, He leads us along a path that points unerringly to that grand spectacle soon to be revealed in God's Son. The books of Exodus and Leviticus, most notably, are replete with sharp allusions to God's redemptive plan, and the tabernacle, with its magnificent unfolding, gives us an object lesson about God's saving grace. The Law, civil and ceremonial, transcribed by Moses, served to instruct consciences and circumscribe behavior until the Fulfiller of the Law should come.

The Law as Schoolmaster

Paul, the former Pharisee, schooled thoroughly in its understanding, described the Law as a "schoolmaster" whose function was "to bring us unto Christ, that we might be justified by faith" (Galatians 3:24). The term *schoolmaster* is not the best translation for the Greek word *paidagogos*, from which we get the English word *pedagogy*. The pedagogue in ancient Greek society did not actually teach lessons to children; instead, this household slave saw to it that they learned the lessons. The pedagogue, the household slave to the householder's son, would attend to the child and supervise the child's nurturance. In his informed study of ancient education, E. B. Castle describes the role of the pedagogue:

> This attendant . . . attended the young master throughout the day. His formal duties were to accompany the boy to and from school, to carry his satchel and to protect him from the pupils of the way. . . . The *paidagogos* was also expected to supervise the young man's manners in the home and in the street and even in school, where he sat in attendance as a symbol of paternal authority throughout the school day. The moral supervision of the *paidagogos* must be stressed . . . the *paidagogos* taught him how to behave.[5]

In the heavily pedagogical Old Testament, God used the experiences of Israel illustratively to prepare the world for the full manifestation in His Son; things that happened to that nation, which can profit us, have been selectively included in the Scriptures (1 Corinthians 10:11). The pedagogical dimension involves two aspects of instruction—practice and precept. Instruction by practice involves the observation of the act. Before Israel, God displayed the lessons in the most minute detail. All the senses were involved: Sounds, sights, smells, as well as touch and movement reinforced the lessons head and heart must learn. The second aspect of *paidagogos* involved precept—the spoken word. All good instruction, as every trained teacher knows, includes both precept and practice.

G. Campbell Morgan's name is legendary to a generation that has profited from the intense labors of many diligent students and gifted teachers of God's Word. Morgan's expositions of the Bible crackle with the fire his untiring inquiry has kindled. As the "prince of Bible teachers," his masterful study of the Gospels would alone accord him a place of prominence among the great Bible teachers. His prodigious writing (based on his public teaching ministry) provide a rich repository of the most insightful and stimulating studies of Scripture. Internationally acclaimed, Morgan traveled the world in his teaching ministry. In addition to pastoral ministries and conference speaking, he also held academic appointments in Great Britain and the United States. Dr. Morgan often publicly appreciated and acknowledged the influence of his early teacher, Joseph Butler, headmaster of Gratton House, where the young Morgan studied. Butler was both preceptor and example for the young men under his care. By referring to him as a "born teacher," his students meant "he was only really happy when he was teaching boys."[6] Under Butler's mentoring, Morgan developed his skills in exegesis and exposition. When Butler died, Morgan wrote to his widow: "Of your beloved husband, I can only think and speak with profound thankfulness and respect which amounts almost to veneration. He was to me one of God's great men. Surely he wore through all the years, the white flower of a blameless life. In the unveilings of the life beyond, he will be told how great his influence has been. I owe him much, and I love him."[7]

Learning and Growth

Cognitive psychologist Jerome Bruner has identified three modes of learning, which he suggests should be employed progressively as the learner matures and advances.[8] Initially, the young learner learns "enactively," primarily acquiring experience through motion and sensation. A curriculum becomes, literally, a walk through a course. In the second, or "iconic," mode pictures and visual imagery replace at some points and supplement at others the initial enactive mode. Last, the emergence of the "symbolic" mode, freed from the dependency upon "concreteness," becomes its own interpreter. The symbol provides greater flexibility than the senses themselves, because the symbol allows a richer repertoire of new ideas to be generated from and associated with it. For example, the "altar" which is, at first, defined in the activity of sacrifice eventually becomes an "icon"—an image that pictures the act of sacrifice. The symbol of sacrifice, no longer tied to the actual altar, generalizes to any service representing the original sacrificial activity. The Old Testament, especially in its literary expression, develops the spiritual truths in a fashion akin to Bruner's modes and presents a fertile framework upon which the New Testament can draw.

We may compare growth in the Christian life to Bruner's stages. Believers are not fully formed at birth. They move through stages and sequences as they change and develop. The apostles Peter and Paul speak about babes in Christ who need food and exercise (Hebrews 5:13, 14; 1 Peter 2:2). Gradually, through time and experience, maturity marks the phases of development. At first we learn of Christ, as it were, through our spiritual senses; we touch and taste and move about in Him. Then we deal with images and representations: We need the examples of other people to follow. We need patterns marked out for us. From the experiences of others, we learn and gain strength to move forward in our own lives. Finally, we come to the stage in which

God speaks to us through His Spirit and His Word. We have what the apostle John calls "an unction from the Holy One" (1 John 2:20). Paul describes a believer at this stage as "the spiritual man" (*see* 1 Corinthians 2:15). When we reach this place, we have moved from the natural to the new, from the carnal to the spiritual.

Our Lord followed a similar pattern in His development into manhood. He did not bypass the legitimate and logical sequence from infancy to adulthood. British author Geoffrey Bull underscores the naturalness of this growth in Christ's life:

> First as the infant in His mother's arms, then as the perfect child. Not that He was unchildlike but that the form of His childhood was perfectly conducive to His normal development on earth. . . . In His continued subjection to His parents at the age of twelve, the most suitable form of life was fully maintained. . . . The godly home, not the temple with its den of thieves was the right environment. Continued childhood and growing into normal youth was the form which the life within Him was bound to prefer. So He grows to the form of His manhood with its manual labor, and its business responsibilities and the care of His mother and sisters. The life of Christ entered on its public form, continuing to its matchless fruition in the purposes of the Cross.[9]

The Lord Jesus, schooled as He was in the tradition and truth of the Old Testament, seized upon that imagery and filled it with His own completeness. By His own admission, He came not to set aside, abrogate, or destroy the Law, but in Himself, to fulfill it (fill it full) (Matthew 5:17). He took the tangible forms and filled them with transcendent truth.

Jesus' appearance at the age of twelve in the Temple gave evidence of His prodigy. A simple schoolboy (it seemed), from the provincial town of Nazareth, where no center of learning existed, mingled with the learned men of the Law. He was not a mere boyish bystander, occasionally contributing a comment or two. As Luke accurately records, He was "sitting in the midst of the doctors, both hearing them, and asking them questions" (Luke 2:46). Anyone else presuming to engage in dialogue with such exalted company they would have rightly considered most blatantly audacious. He was God incarnate; yet undeniably, He was also Man (as Luke, with his quick eye for the truly human, tells us) growing in symmetry and balance in all areas of life (Luke 2:52). This youth among the ancients—this pupil among the professors—had devoted Himself to the demanding task of learning, which at every stage of His development was His "Father's business" for Him. Nurtured away from public scrutiny, in the obscurity of Galilee, our Lord then emerged and embarked upon His public ministry of teaching. At the Jordan River, when John baptized him, heaven opened and acknowledged this divinely anointed and appointed One. The gentle dove of innocence descended and abode upon Him. In confirmation, the Voice came from glory, testifying that those years in Galilee well pleased God (Luke 3:21, 22).

Endued with power, the blessed Christ, in dovelike demeanor, was led by the Spirit to His first public test. The most merciless scrutiny of His mettle for forty days would mark this critical examination. All heaven witnessed this intense interrogation. He dared not undertake any teaching to any audience until the time of His own audience had come. ". . . Tempted of the devil" (Luke 4:2): the adversarial encounter! Although sent from heaven, He could not teach on earth until, through the ultimate assessment, He demonstrated wisdom, skill, knowledge, and integrity. The consummate confrontation! Relying solely upon references from the Word of God, without the employment of any prerogatives of deity, the tested One emerged victorious as the devil retreated.

Christ, the Master-Teacher, entered upon His public ministry. He is the fulfillment of Isaiah's prophecy (Luke 4:21). Teaching and touching would fill His days. For three energetic years, He moved among the people and taught them about God. His schedule was so full and His activities so numerous that "if they should be written every one . . . the world itself could not contain the books that should be written" (John 21:25).

4
WORDS FOR MANKIND

This book of the law shall not depart out of thy mouth; but thou shalt meditate therein day and night, that thou mayest observe to do according to all that is written therein: for then thou shalt make thy way prosperous, and then thou shalt have good success.

Joshua 1:8

Reading on wise and virtuous subjects is, next to prayer, the best improvement of our hearts. It enlightens us, calms us, collects our thoughts, and prompts us to better efforts. We say that a man is known by the friends he keeps; but a man is known better by his many books.[1]

Except a living man, there is nothing more wonderful than a book! . . . We ought to reverence books, to look at them as useful and mighty things. If they are good and true . . . they are the messages of Christ. . . .[2]

I recently read a sad statistic. Numbers generally do not make me maudlin, but I came near to tears when I found that women buy the most books in Christian bookstores. Don't get me wrong. I'm not against women, women readers, or women book buyers; but it does disturb me that other people do not read. More frightening, the statistics stated that the least likely person to buy a book was a clergyman. Astounding! If that fearful prospect of nonreading clergy is remotely accurate, the church faces a spiritual famine. I could only find it more frightening that teachers might not read (unimaginable)! A nonreading teacher seems a contradiction in terms.

Why Read?

A mild disclaimer is in order as we approach the topic of literacy. Obviously, we cannot learn certain things from books. The pragmatists among us delight in repeating that tiresome refrain of conventional wisdom. However, some things (many things!) can *only* be learned from books; they enlarge myriad pleasures and pastimes. Abraham Lincoln, asked what he considered the most important invention, without hesitation, replied: "the written word."[3] If all our books were destroyed, civilization would be back at the starting point.

In His first public teaching, Jesus used a book. Returning to Nazareth, the city of His own schooldays, He attended the synagogue and ". . . stood up for to read. And there was delivered unto him the book . . ." (Luke 4:16, 17). Of course that meant the Bible—the Book of all books! At the outset of His teaching ministry, our Lord unapologetically identified Himself as someone who was familiar with and in favor of books. Schooled in the Old Testament Scriptures, Christ quoted them spontaneously on numerous occasions. Because He had filled Himself with their teaching, by long, painstaking hours of diligent study, He knew them well. His knowledge of prophetic events that surrounded His life and His awareness of their fulfillment in His actions came from His understanding of Scripture.

As the career of the apostle Paul drew to its close and soon he would die under the executioner's blade, what last requests did that prisoner make? As he wrote to his "son in the faith," Timothy, he identified the priorities in his life. When you come, he told Timothy, ". . . bring . . . the books, . . . especially the parchments" (2 Timothy 4:13). Paul had been a lifelong reader. Acquainted alike with the Hebraic and Hellenistic, he was, as Francis Bacon has characterized all who read, "a full man." In earlier correspondence Paul encouraged Timothy to "give attendance to reading" (1 Timothy 4:13). Paul did not view books as luxuries of the self-indulgent; they were the indispensable resources for any serious student. Christian students, above all, need to be serious.

The sage Solomon assures us "of making many books there is no end" (Ecclesiastes 12:12). A recent story of a man who almost lost his life because of his love for books humorously substantiates that statement. An eighty-six-year-old resident of a California coastal town was nearly buried alive for hours under six tons of books. The volumes, lining the walls of his room and stacked from floor to ceiling, tumbled down upon him when an earthquake shocked southern California.[4]

Often critics have interpreted Solomon's remark as a cynical commentary on the futility of reading and studying. To me this seems an unfair appraisal. Solomon, in philosophical reflection, realizes that books are efforts to ferret out and fathom truth, exercises (of varying worth, admittedly) in discovering and distilling knowledge. All books, whether traditional treatises, scientific inquiries, or poetic expressions, make statements about life and its meaning. Though we may debate their quality and challenge their ultimate contributions, that does not detract from the venture each author undertook in telling his tale. The writing of books has no end, because the quest of the human soul for solutions to the enigmas of life never ends. The need to search the vast universe, to discover and uncover, is part of the insatiable spiritual appetite that must feed or famish. God delights to hide things, the Scripture tells us, and it is "the honour of kings . . . to search out a matter" (Proverbs 25:2). All who seek to explore the vastness of the knowledge God has given involve themselves in kingly business. Royalty writes and reads books. "Reading is a weariness to the flesh," Solomon concluded at the end of his vain and cynical search for wisdom (*see* Ecclesiastes 12:12), but his evaluation was that of a man "under the sun," where nothing seemed to make sense. Reading seems wearisome because good reading takes good time, but all good tasks are hard, and as Elton Trueblood learned, "prime tasks require prime time."[5]

The Joy of Reading

My few favorite places have always included libraries. Next to churches (I confess even more so at times), libraries have provided me with the cool comfort of unhurried ease. As C. S. Lewis delighted in Grundy Library, "Not only because it was a library, but because it was a sanctuary,"[6] so have I enjoyed such homes of books. Libraries refresh me the way one teacher refreshed her students in Georgia. Unable to free themselves from the provincialism of their locale, by the magic of their teacher's storytelling, the children traveled to distant worlds in flights of fancy and were transported beyond the limitations of their meager lives.[7]

The only public library in my town fittingly faced the elementary school—a short distance across the street, but those few steps spanned ages. When I walked inside those book-lined walls, I had carte blanche to a tantalizing array of adventure and lore. In a town where privation prevailed, *in libris* provided temporary exemption from the harshness of a world gone mad. No one refused me admittance, and the cheerful countenance of the librarian said: *You are welcome here*. I confess a sense of sentimentality when I think of libraries. I am not too partial to modern buildings, with their plastic paneling and textureless interiors. I remember creosote-soaked, creaking floorboards, heavy with the weight of miles of words; light filtering through opaque windows; dust particles dancing in suspension; the stale smells of parchment, musty and mysterious; and the spectral solitude in a world of hushed reverence.

In contemporary times when mass communication discourages the leisure reading requires, we may shortchange ourselves if we capitulate to other modes and neglect books. Books allow us to ponder and contemplate. They never rush or force themselves upon us. They are servants responsive to our reading whims. If we miss the message the first time, we simply reread. If we failed at first sighting, we re-view. God in great wisdom has committed His communication to us in His written Word. Next to the unmediated revelation in Christ Jesus, the mediated revelation in the Bible is our greatest treasure. We have access to God's Word. What an illustrious literary lineage has been sired by this single Book! Within the English-speaking world particularly, the Scriptures have provided unparalleled literacy. Countless stories of changed lives testify to the Bible's impact. A recent publication has summarized the books that have influenced the influential. Leaders, past and present, within the Christian community have given their judgments about special books that have affected them significantly, and one section identifies thoughts about the Bible, specifically, and the testimonials to it.[8]

The Master Book, when disregarded, will witness to lives damaged and destroyed. An education that ignores God's Word is an education in name only. In his Lyman Beecher Lectures, given at Yale University, James Stewart faced the issue forthrightly and refused to compromise the role of the Word of God in any education enterprise that calls itself Christian:

> How urgent this task now is may be illustrated from
> a remark made in a recent discussion on Bible instruc-
> tion in the schools: "Let us teach them the ideals of
> the Fatherhood of God and the brotherhood of man—

but that is all: the Christian rudiments—none of your supernatural accretions, none of your sectarian theology.'' An alarming revelation surely of the confusion that can exist even in Christian minds! What right have we—for the sake of an educational syllabus, or for anything else—to define a Christianity in terms which implicitly deny the presuppositions of every sentence the men of the New Testament wrote?[9]

The Power of the Written Word

During my undergraduate college days, I delivered a persuasive speech entitled ''The Pen Is Mightier Than the Sword.'' I tried to demonstrate that books have had a more potent impact upon the course of the world's events than wars. The wars themselves, I contended, had origins in ideas the books propagated. Hitler's *Mein Kampf* became his own mandate for the emergence of the Nazi party in Germany and his maniacal efforts to subjugate Europe. The *Communist Manifesto*, written by Karl Marx, became the creed of Lenin and precipitated the Russian Revolution. Three great philosophical and ideological revolutions of the Western world have been attributed to writings that reformulated the conception of mankind. Copernicus's views elevated the heliocentric view of the solar system and subordinated the role planet Earth played and ''struck a narcissistic blow at man's pride by forcing him to take a less grandiose view of himself.'' This was the ''cosmological'' revolution. Darwin's epochal *Origin of Species* and *Descent of Man* reduced mankind further in the scheme of things and placed him among the ''lower'' animal species. This was the ''biological'' revolution. In the twentieth century, Sigmund Freud dealt the final blow, and his iconoclastic writings ''shattered illusions about the infallibility of human reason and conscience, the existence of free will and the essential purity of human nature.'' The psychological revolution had dealt the death blow.[10]

But books have had an equally potent—and perhaps an incalculably greater—influence for good. Crusades and quests have been undertaken as a result of chance readings of books. Reading prompted Don Quixote's strangely comical quest for the "unreachable star."

> You must know then, that when our gentleman had nothing to do (which was almost all the year round), he passed his time in reading books of knight-errantry . . . he sold many acres of arable land to purchase books of that kind . . . he gave himself up wholly to the reading of romances that a-nights he would pore on until it was day, and a-days he would read on until it was night; and thus, by sleeping little and reading much, the moisture of his brain was exhausted.[11]

Preoccupation with certain books, to the point of bibliomania, might produce unhealthy states of mind, but I doubt it causes lack of brain moisture! From the launching pads of books many a spirit has soared. Missionary stories have fired the imagination and fueled the efforts of generations of pioneers in God's service. Jim Elliot, slaving over Greek and patristics at Wheaton College, read voraciously and regularly recorded his thoughts and desires in his diary.[12] Serendipitous encounters with books have ignited lives that burned brilliantly for God. Hudson Taylor, legendary in the annals of missionary movements, traces his exploits to a single book—a seemingly accidental choice of readings from his father's library. Taylor's son tells how it all began:

> The beginning of it all was a quiet hour among his father's books, when young Hudson Taylor sought something to interest him. His mother was away from home and the boy was missing her. The house seemed so empty, so he took the story he found to a favorite corner in the old warehouse, thinking he would read it as long as it did not get prosy.
> . . . The boy was reading, meanwhile, the booklet he had picked up, and as the story merged into something more serious, he was arrested by the words: "The finished work of Christ. . . ."

Old doubts and fears were gone. The reality of the wonderful experience we call conversion filled him with peace and joy.[13]

C. S. Lewis has emerged as one of the major Christian apologists of this era. His writings continue to be extremely popular, and he is frequently cited as the most penetrating, articulate, and provocative thinker and writer on the contemporary Christian scene. Adept in a variety of literary genres, he never sacrificed honesty or scholarship for style. His writings possess "that hyperborean crispness, stringency, and charm as of a well-braced musical instrument" (to use a Thomas Hardy phrase). Lewis spent his early life encased in books. Both his father and mother read avidly. When Lewis was seven years old, his father built a large house and this new house became, for Lewis, "a major character" in his life story.

I am the product of long corridors, empty sunlit rooms, upstairs indoor silences, attics explored in solitude. . . . Also, of endless books. My father bought all the books he read and never got rid of any of them. There were books in the study, books in the drawing room, books in the cloakroom (two deep) in the great bookcase on the landing, books in the bedroom, books piled as high as my shoulder in the cistern attic, books of all kinds reflecting every transient stage of my parents' interest, books readable and unreadable, books suitable for a child and books most emphatically not. Nothing was forbidden me.[14]

G. K. Chesterton and George MacDonald profoundly influenced Lewis's pilgrimage in the Christian faith. Of Chesterton's book *The Everlasting Man*, Lewis writes: "Then I read Chesterton's Everlasting Man and for the first time saw the whole Christian outline of history set out in a form that seemed to make sense."[15] In fact, Lewis acknowledged George MacDonald as "my master" and confessed he had never written a book in which he did not quote from him. The novel *Phantastes* "left the deepest and most enduring impression on both his literary and his spiritual life."[16]

Lewis held strong opinions about the benefit of books and showed partiality to "old books," by which he meant those treatises that have lasted. They are the true grain that have withstood the winnowing of the winds of time that have swept away the merely fashionable and faddish chaff. Such enduring classics, he contends, correct the myopic misconceptions and limitations of the present. "Every age has its own outlook. . . . We all, therefore, need the books that will correct the characteristic mistakes of our own period. And that means the old books. . . . The only palliative is to keep the clean sea breeze of the centuries blowing through our minds, and this can be done only by reading old books."[17]

Of course, Lewis did not offhandedly dismiss all modern writing. That would preclude all contemporary insights, including those found in his writings. But each generation's errors appear more readily when we contrast them to the ripened vintage of prior ages.

The Dangers of Books

As a teacher, I know the truth of which Lewis speaks and the strong temptation to be beguiled by the novelty of current thought. Thoughts expressed need the tempering that time can give them, and we need to establish firm literary linkages between the vitality of recent writings and the maturity of time-honored truth. A book is a dangerous thing! When Hilkiah the priest discovered the Book of the Law in the refuse pile within the Temple and had it read to King Josiah, revival broke out in the land (2 Chronicles 34:14–33). Lewis's own conversion could not have occurred apart from the books he read. Intractable in his atheism, he seemed an unlikely recruit for the forces of righteousness. He guarded his pagan ways with scrupulous oversight. But the unexpected occurred and God's witness came in the guise of a book: "In reading Chesterton, as in reading MacDonald, I did not know what I was letting myself in for. A young man who wishes to remain a sound Atheist cannot be too careful of his reading. There are traps everywhere—Bibles laid open, millions of surprises . . . fine nets and strategems. God is, if I may say it, very unscrupulous.''[18]

Sometimes the danger of indiscriminate reading feeds us a ''husk diet'' of books that malnourish us. Good books, like good nutrition, should give us an enlarged capacity and keener appetite for quality. A daily diet of processed reading, with all the vitamins and nutrients stripped away, will give us a bloated, full feeling, while leaving us empty in the inner man. Perennially appealing books provide a storehouse of undiminished resources we can draw upon for information and inspiration. A British sociologist cautions against the allure of insipid and superficial reading:

> What is particularly dismaying is that not only does the flood of publications reveal an abundance of pompous bluff and a paucity of new ideas, but even the old and valuable insights which we have inherited from our illustrious ancestors are being drowned in a torrent of meaningless verbiage. . . . Pretentious and nebulous verbosity, interminable repetition of platitudes and disguised propaganda are the order of the day.[19]

A Nobel-Prize-winning physicist who worked on the historic Manhattan Project echos these sentiments particularly as he laments about the textbooks he reviewed for his local school system. In these books that found their way into public schools, he found gross errors in the math books and a scarcity of applied science in science books. In one instance that strained credulity to the limits, the publisher sent a textbook with entirely blank pages for examination and possible adoption. In order to make the school board's review deadline, even though the book was not completed, the publisher sent a volume—with no words—to fulfill the technicality of meeting the date.[20]

The Benefits of Books

In leading them along the road of good reading, teachers do their students a great favor. Good reading begets good reading.

Worthwhile books lead to other worthwhile books. I can trace a genealogy in my successive reading of good books which has at each new generation of reading given birth to an even better book. The purer the line in literature, the less probability that one will encounter a runt in the litter. We would do well to heed the words of John Bunyan: "My readers, I have something else to do, than with vain stories trouble you; Let no man then count me a fable-maker, nor make my name or credit a partaker of their derision; what is here in view, of mine own knowledge, I dare say is true."[21]

To be *religious* in the finest sense of the word is to read. Cicero contended that the root of the word *religion* (*religio*) originally meant the continual reading and rereading of the sacred books. Scottish theologian Alexander Whyte equates the religious man with the man who reads good books that enoble and inspire the life of faith. The Christian teacher who seeks to see his students grow in that life must nurture belief through the reading of believable books. Whyte tells us, "True religion, even in its etymology, stands firm and fruitful in the continual reading of the Word of God, till that Word dwells richly in the assiduous reader's mind and heart."[22]

The great genius of man is his God-given capacity for language and literacy. No other species within the animal world leaves a written record for posterity. Books are the joyful means by which each generation tells about itself, keeps faith with its ancestry, and shares with its posterity. Down the centuries, dating from the Master-Teacher's message, inscriptions have passed on all worthwhile knowledge. God-breathed words constitute Holy Writ, and multitudes of manuscripts have come from the second wind—the breathings of those He has breathed upon. The luxuriant legacy of literacy must ever be the teacher's treasure and the student's storehouse. Asked what he would sacrifice in his labors, a missionary who worked in a simple setting, laboring in the jungle of South America responded, "I would gladly part with everything I have, except—" He paused meditatively. "Except my books. Take all other possessions, but leave my books. Books are my bloodline."

— Part II —
THE
EXCELLENT
TEACHER

We all know a good teacher when we see one, but it's hard to put a finger on just what it takes to be one. What does the one who stands head and shoulders above the rest— the excellent teacher—do that's different from the others? Where does the inspiration come from?

5
DRAWING NEAR

. . . Yet shall not thy teachers be removed into a corner
any more, but thine eyes shall see thy teachers.

Isaiah 30:20

Many a boy whose home life was a morass of untidiness
and improvisation because his parents were not house
trained, has escaped from it and shaped his own character
and career satisfactorily, because he admired and imitated a
teacher whose life was orderly and yet humane and satisfying. [1]

In ancient mythology, before he left for Troy, Odysseus (the forever-after symbol of the eternal quest of man) gave his son, Telemachus, into the care of Mentor, whom he charged with looking after the household and attending to Telemachus's educational needs. Thus *mentor* has become a term that speaks of closeness and kindness in education.

Discovering a Mentor

Even if we surround ourselves with many acquaintances, we keep tight the inner circle into which we permit intimates; trusted friends are few. In the same way, though we all have known many teachers, not many can own the mantle of the mentor. The bond that knits itself between student and teacher requires an affinity that develops only during protracted times of soul kinship.

How many students ever find their "true" teacher-mentor? I saw it happen in a graduate sociology class during the 1960s, when students wore their rebellion on their sleeves, daring professor and pundit alike to rip it off. The class was large—about seventy students in the lecture hall. The professor—a knowledgeable, original, articulate, and understandable lecturer—had a national reputation in sociological theory. In contrast to the rest of us, two students with unkempt hair, wiry beards, and disheveled appearance stood out. During the opening weeks of the term, they behaved with belligerence bordering on defiance. The professor parried the blows, retorted in kind when necessary, but generally remained controlled and reasoned in his remarks. During that term, I observed a transformation taking place in those two students: Their comments became increasingly more courteous, and the repartee betrayed a growing camaraderie. After the term ended, I saw neither student for more than a year. As I strolled across campus one day, I met the more militant of the two and scarcely recognized him. His hair was fashionably styled, his attire more conservative, and his demeanor less abrasive. We talked a bit, and I asked if he had had any more courses with that teacher. "Oh yes," he remarked. "I'm his graduate assistant, and he's directing my dissertation now." The professor had become his mentor.

The Mentor-Teacher

Unlike the situation in schools, where students may seek out a mentor and not find one, Jesus has sought out those He would teach. For those whom He has called Jesus Christ is *the* Mentor, the Master-Teacher above all others.

Principally the mentor wants to *influence* others; he wants to impact lives entrusted to his care. He seeks to form character, mold manners, and leave firm impressions, just as our Lord did with the disciples. Jesus called twelve to "be with him" (Mark 3:14). Then, in close proximity, He nurtured and developed their capacities and enlarged their horizons. Rather than reducing the disciples to an indistinguishable blob (a frightening prospect for students) Christ respected their distinctiveness and individuality. His teaching made the most of them, and today He does the same with us.

What joy for a teacher to know that he or she has influenced lives, and what vitality it can give to a teaching career! One school teacher who contemplated retirement had second thoughts when he received this letter from a thankful student: "I'll miss you very much next year, but I won't forget anything you've taught me. I hope you know what a mentor you are for me, as well as for many others, I'm sure. I also hope that you'll continue to do what you do for high-school students because you have such a significant influence in my life."[2]

Jesus was no garden-variety teacher who spouted aphorisms as fancy struck him. He attracted His hearers by deftly combining the deliberate and the spontaneous. In the select circle of His confidants He charmed and changed lives. The parables He gave to the large crowds, but He clarified the interpretations to that small group inside the house. After His resurrection from the dead, upon the disciples in the upper room Jesus breathed the Holy Spirit (John 20:22). The Mentor-Teacher breathes life (*inspires*, in the literal sense) into His students. They are never beyond His breath's infilling. Closely huddled near the Mentor, they catch and delight in the aromatic delicacy of every breathless word.

The Touching Teacher

I have watched young children huddle around their teachers, clinging securely to them, seeking affection from them. Early in the school year, most children crave close contact with teachers. Children new to school are drawn with unabashed attachment, and it seems natural for them to bask in their teacher's physical presence. Only after years of rebuff do students form a circle quite distant from the teacher, and the circle widens until it becomes all circumference, with no center at all. Parading around the pedagogical periphery, students in junior and senior high school begin to cling to one another instead. The soft extension of the teacher in early years erodes as rigidity hardens the teacher away from students, and tangible connections drop off as the space becomes greater and greater. Discouraged youngsters seek to close the gap in a circle of peer relationships, which can never provide any solid center for human consensus.

Mentor-teachers are tactual in temperament, always within touching range. Their sweet breath of bonding forms a spiritual zone of support. The twelve moved within the close circle of Christ's presence and seldom left His sight. He did not lecture to them as He did the crowds. Subtle gestures spoke volumes— nuances of voice, a glance, postural cues. The Mentor-Teacher is a master with small groups.

I have been extensively involved with small-group sessions where members have close contact. These intimate contexts enhance nonverbal communication. At times, body language expresses more than words. Space between participants may widen or reduce as trust grows or shrinks. Expansive, accepting body gestures signal support, or rigid postures tell participants to keep their distance. In a circle of few, signs of uneasiness become more difficult to hide. Apprehension and apathy are less easily disguised; attention and acceptance are more readily detected. Teachers trained in interpersonal dynamics utilize small-group mentoring techniques to foster openness and growth. Vital interactions in nonthreatening small groups can encourage previously reluctant students to disclose themselves and find support from their peers.

A vivid reminder of the power of mentoring programs comes from a teaching experience in one of my college classes. I divided the class into small groups and instructed group members to probe each other for growth goals. In this kind of "grill session" no one was allowed to sit complacently uninvolved. One female student burst into tears and wept almost uncontrollably. Another group member took her hand and held it firmly, without speaking. Finally the tears subsided, the student gained her composure and poise, and began to talk about some personal problems she had never shared with anyone. The group cohesiveness that developed, even in that short time, gave her enough support to deal with her own previously unconfronted feelings. Some tears, an opportunity to ventilate, uncritical acceptance—all gave her a growth change in her life.

The Listening Teacher

Jesus, the Mentor-Teacher, listens as well as speaks. He listens attentively and authentically. Listening may range from superficial, indulgent listening to the profound, responsive hearing—listening with the "third ear." At the time of Lazarus's death (John 11), Jesus listened to Martha's strident, annoyed remarks and responded accordingly: He met words with words. Mary, on the other hand, said almost nothing to the Savior, but her tears spoke volumes, and He replied in kind: "Jesus wept" (v. 35).

How remarkably close to Christ the apostle John got! Do we consider the accessibility of the Lord and especially the tactual closeness observed and recorded by John? *That* disciple heard the heartbeat of Jesus! Around the eating table at the Last Supper, with Judas and John, respectively, on the right and left of Jesus, conversation flowed among them and so close was the contact that others could not fully understand words said by Peter to John and words said by Jesus to Judas (John 13:21–30).

The woman at the well did not receive a lecture. The Mentor-Teacher converses casually; He does not intimidate or alienate. Disregarding rabbinical tradition, He allows her close enough for Him to learn details about her life that she had successfully hidden from her few friends. The Mentor will not shout or lift up His voice. You must come close enough to hear. Tutorials are made for moments like these.

Proximity between tutor and apprentice is a potent force for all learning. We may inversely relate the distance between teacher and student to learning: less space, more learning; larger space, lean learning. Students at Magdalen College, Oxford, eagerly sought C. S. Lewis. Enrollment in his tutorial was an academic prize reserved for a few select ones. His winsome manner, "impetuous cordiality," and massive presence elevated him to mentor status: "To have C. S. Lewis as a tutor was universally regarded as an awesome honor."[3]

I had just entered seventh grade, and the electricity of adolescence surged through me. My elementary school days had been eventful, but not particularly promising. During these junior-high-school years, I would need direction. My intellectual and emotional capacities were charged, but without harnessing, they would burn themselves out, unproductively, in undisciplined, youthful profligacy.

Early in the year, my homeroom teacher placed his arm around me—more avuncular than paternal—and cautioned me against my perilous course. "I can see the direction you're headed," he said firmly. "I see a lot before you, and if you choose not to change, there's disaster up ahead. You have ability—the record shows it. This school is a new start, but it will, if you persist, be the same old finish. You've got too much going for you to waste yourself. Give yourself a chance. We're here to help, but that's all we can do. We can't run your life. I'm telling you while it's still early. Do something before it's too late."

I probably feigned indifference (juvenile nonchalance), but I thought seriously about his advice. We became fast friends, that teacher and I, for those three remaining school years. I'm sure at times, subsequent to that talk, he thought it didn't sink in, but when I moved to high school, my academic bearings were on course and my emotional resources creatively under control. One mentor had intervened and altered a schoolboy's life. Perhaps the most rewarding words a teacher can hear are the words said by a student in later life: "Remember what you said to me when I was in your class? I never forgot those words."

The Selective Teacher

On several occasions, Jesus took His disciples into a cloistered place of confidence, where He spoke to them alone. At times, only John, James, and Peter were privy to the special teaching the Lord gave. On the Mount of Transfiguration and in the sanctuary of Gethsemane, a stone's throw from the others, this trio viewed two separate and special spectacles. On the Mount, the Transfiguration revealed the inherent glory of Christ and permitted His deity, previously veiled, to radiate. In the garden, the contrasting temptation revealed His essential humanity as bloodlike drops of sweat oozed through broken skin. In the first scene, God the Father talked from heaven to the Son; in the second, God the Son on earth talked to His Father. On the Mount, the Father declared: "This is my beloved Son: hear him" (Mark 9:7). In the garden, the Son, in prayerful petition to the Father, acknowledged that He was always heard by the Father (John 17). On both occasions, within that intensely private penumbra of the Mentor-Teacher's sphere of sacred converse, He reserved the dialogue between deity for those three only. In later years, after James's martyrdom (Acts 12:2), Peter and John would serve valiantly in the vanguard of the corps of teachers who themselves mentored other students. They would write Gospels and Epistles that chronicled and continued the lessons begun by the Mentor-Teacher.

Mentor-teachers are keenly aware that all aspects of their lives are open to view and scrutiny of students, and they must limit the size of the "student body." Tutelage cannot succeed in a large class. Small movements, insignificant to a crowd, become properly interpreted when observed firsthand. The mentor primarily aims at having his style and substance transferred to the apprentice. As single cells exchange nuclei when they fuse, tutor and pupil interact, and the tutor imprints himself within his pupil.

Jesus quite selectively chose His disciples who formed the celebrated circle of intimates. Only after an agonizing night of prayer could He call them (Luke 6:12, 13). The disciples would be coached according to the Mentor's game plan. Mentor-teachers choose their students much as a coach of an athletic team chooses his players. Not all contestants have equal capabilities. The sharp eye of the experienced coach makes the fine distinctions among players and the critical difference between champions and losers. But it is always the coach's choice!

In *Chariots of Fire*, the popular, award-winning film, Harold Abrahams, England's celebrated runner, eagerly enlists the services of Europe's most outstanding track coach. In one scene, Abrahams tells the coach he wants to develop a more effective style of running for Olympic competition. The coach appears a bit startled, then smiles. Turning to Abrahams, he says with an amused look: "Like the bridegroom, it's the coach who should do the asking." In other words, the mentor makes the choice! Selection of who sits at the Mentor's table is never the pupil's prerogative; the mentor is never *obligated* to choose anyone. "You have not chosen me, but I have chosen you," Jesus reminded his disciples. There is no incumbency upon Christ!

At higher levels of education (notably graduate school and doctoral programs), this compelling process becomes most visible. Only the most audacious student would assume he could choose his advisor or dissertation chairman. In graduate study, I occasionally observed obsequious behavior by students. Hat in hand, they approached faculty, seeking endorsement. Disturbingly, some faculty would pander to students and encourage such subservience. They seemed to take delight in watching students grovel in the academic dirt. The Lord Jesus would not resort to such demeaning tactics.

The Meek and Merciful Teacher

Above all, a student needs the trait of "teachableness" to profit from close instruction with the mentor-teacher. The Bible terms it "meekness." On a campus graffiti board at one university, someone had written: "The meek shall inherit the earth." Underneath those words, a student had scrawled: "If it's all right with everyone." Unfortunately, that sentiment seems to sum up the persistent definition assigned to *meekness*.

People often equate meekness with "weakness" and, of course, see weakness as the major liability in life. But that definition is far afield. In reality, weakness and meekness stand poles apart; only the strong are capable of true meekness, which requires the disciplined direction of strength. The meek student under the mentor's tutelage harnesses abilities and channels them productively into specified and worthwhile accomplishments. Students who lack meekness squander their little strength as it dissipates in bursts of restlessness and unregulated activity.

Our Lord, in His single, self-descriptive statement, identified Himself as "meek and lowly in heart" (Matthew 11:29). Christ knew that effectiveness and fruitfulness in the disciples' future ministry were strategically aligned with the development of meekness. Meekness linked Jesus with one of the most effective leaders in the Bible. The Scriptures call Moses the "meekest man on the face of the earth" (*see* Numbers 12:3). He became God's duly ordained leader in the most important phase of the nation of Israel's life. The exodus from Egypt and the subsequent forty years in the wilderness imposed on Moses the awesome responsibility of leading a nation of more than 2 million people. Meekness characterized Moses' leadership. During the previous forty years in desert obscurity, Moses learned (under God's tutelage) the skill that allowed him to lead the vast, undisciplined array. Moses—the name spoken by generations of Jews, with hushed and holy reverence—towered above his contemporaries, dwarfed the ruler of Egypt, and remained meek. Moses' forte was leadership.

Any who dare to lead (as teachers must) will be challenged to demonstrate, convincingly, that the covering of mercy canopies their lives. Few things have more danger than power in the hands of unregulated despots. God does not choose His leaders for their aggressiveness or their skills in intimidation. Under the maturing grace of meekness, Moses had been mentored with godly civility. When the temptation toward self-assertion surfaced, the moderating balance wheel of meekness regained stability and equilibrium. Even on those occasions when Moses slipped from beneath the canopy of meekness, quick recognition saved him (and Israel) from peril.

Two Greek words are generally translated "gentleness" or "meekness" in the Bible. *Tapeinophrosune* is normally translated "humility," "meekness," "gentleness," or "lowliness" in the King James Version. *Praotes* is more often the preferred word for "meekness."[4] Matthew 11:29 uses both terms to describe the Lord Jesus. In classical Greek usage, Aristotle's definition of *praotes* is an inviting one: "In discussing meekness, he said it is that which stands between *orgiotees* (excessive anger) and *aorgeesia*, (angerlessness). . . . It is neither constant anger nor total absence of anger, but seasoned controlled anger."[5]

Meekness, therefore, involves not a passive acquiescence to events that come into our lives, nor does it indicate a passionless indifference to their impact. The Bible advocates nothing of the Eastern mystic's apathy. Meekness is synonymous with neither cowering, spineless, docile spirit nor impulsive, impassioned recklessness. The Lord Jesus did not allow anyone to violate His person without His permission, nor was He incapable of godly anger. When He twice cleansed the Temple, He displayed an unmistakable displeasure (John 2:13–17; Matthew 21:12, 13). No emotionless Messiah purged the sanctuary.

Meekness constitutes a conscious balance between extremes and excesses and permits (indeed encourages) appropriate displays of anger and concern in the presence of evil and unbelief. Like a precisely angled laser, whose controlled beam penetrates what in its dissipated form it only illuminated, meekness in the Mentor-Teacher is the manageable and spontaneous display of righteous indignation. But Moses had to learn meekness that would make him amenable to God's guidance. Interestingly, Moses had benefited from the finest schooling of his day in the nation of Egypt. The most prestigious faculty in the fabled land of constant wonder taught him. World-renowned for engineering spectacles and marvels of architecture, ancient Egypt continues to dazzle the modern world. Yet Moses never learned meekness in the schools of the world. In those halls of learning, power and human potential dominated; they mockingly relegated meekness to the margins; it was not part of the desideratum. Contemporary humanism, which acknowledges no truth beyond its own and makes man "the measure of all things," arrogantly ignores the virtue God deems most useful for His work. Ironically, in the face of seemingly insolvable problems, humanism persists in its intractable arrogance. As David Ehrenfeld states:

> Humanism and modern society have opted albeit unconsciously, for the assumptions of human power. The choice was understandable—the assumptions have long seemed, superficially, to work, and they certainly have been (and still are) gratifying to the ego. Now that the assumptions have manifestly gone sour, many humanists appear bewildered by the paradoxes they have created for themselves. . . . Dehumanization of people . . . destruction of the natural world . . . humanism itself has spawned the apotheosis, worship of the machines and the human-as-imitator of the machine.[6]

A meek spirit comes not through hasty gulps from stagnant pools of past experience but from leisurely draughts from deeply dug wells. Meekness makes us move slowly; the mentor-teacher does not fear taking time to produce quality. Jesus provided no "crash course" for His disciples. The moments he spends with God by the well of the Word, drinking deeply of its life-giving and life-sustaining flow measure a man's meekness. Mentor-teachers' effectiveness relies on their students' willingness to be schooled in the leisure of learning. Aristotle stayed with Plato for more than two decades. The term *school* is derived from the term "leisure" and a *scholar* takes the time needed to learn.

The intensive cross-culture study tours I conduct come as close to a mentor-teacher relationship as any educational experience I have. They provide opportunities to observe saints in relaxed reverence—those who, by their examples, reveal to the hasty Westerner how to develop true godliness. On one trip to Greece, we visited a pastor-teacher who lay in a hospital bed, recuperating from surgery:

> The hospital room was inadequate by American standards—a bed, small table and little else. No television to entertain, no nurses obedient to the slightest beckoning, no modern facilities. We slipped into the room and were greeted by a smiling brother who welcomed us. He caressed his young daughter whom he held affectionately during our hour long conversation. He had time for her and us. . . . As he related his story in calm and contented tones, we were struck by the tranquility of his life and the testimony he bore to the sufficiency of Christ in situations of which many . . . would have despaired. We prayed together, commended each other to the Lord and then we quietly withdrew from the bleak hospital room which had strangely become like a sanctuary.[7]

Pupils who dare to be embraced under the Mentor's mantle must commit themselves to long times of prayer, meditation, and study. There are no shortcuts to sainthood. Outstanding Bible teacher Alan Redpath has declared that salvation is the miracle of a moment, but the making of the man of God takes the labor of a lifetime. There is a justifiable jealousy about mentor-teachers. They insist upon wholehearted and clear-headed allegiance and have little time for the instability of the "double minded man" (James 1:8). Nor will they tolerate indifference. The aspiring applicant to tutelage cannot expect to begin with exhilaration and soon settle comfortably into a routine of convenience. Students who begin with joy, like the seed in the stony place of the parable (Matthew 13:20), and then wilt away would do well to remain in the hothouse atmosphere of academia, where the soil does not require toil. Growth in the garden of the soul will not appear if God cannot cultivate the soil or if it proves unarable.

Mentor-teachers seek ignitable students. Moses turned aside to see the burning bush and by that act declared his own eligibility for ignition (Exodus 3:2). Mentor-teachers take idle sticks and conflagrate them. Jim Elliot, model student and missionary, had an insatiable appetite for knowledge of God and an ignitable spirit, kindled under the Holy Spirit's tutelage. His prayer that God would ignite his life and set him aflame was answered in dramatic fashion upon the altar of God's service.[8]

Christ set the world ablaze with the willing timber of lowly but ignitable lives. Our Lord Jesus, the perfect Man, was continually burning but never burned out. The Gospels relate the life of a Teacher upon whom others made unrelenting demands. Rising early in the morning, He ministered indefatigably to needs, where He met them. The meek One was never consumed.

Meekness is medicinal; like balm, it heals the soul and serves as a perpetual supply of energy. Self-assertion quickly depletes the meager source of energy. The present literature on professional and psychological problems that plague teachers often describes "professional exhaustion syndrome" (or "burnout"). Intense interpersonal relationships, such as mentor-teachers experience, precipitate stress and emotional conflict. Without access to fresh supplies of emotional fuel, teachers become consumed.

Burnout involves a loss of positive feeling for students; teachers begin to see them in depersonalized and dehumanized ways. Typically, they develop that most critical symptom, a kind of cynicism. Is it all worthwhile? "Why should I devote myself to the thankless task of teaching?" the burned-out teacher asks. Such questions become all too frequently repeated. I suspect the best of mentor-teachers have allowed these distasteful notions to cross their minds, and I confess I have had my own moments (days?) of second thoughts. Why a teacher? Sometimes I felt I beat my head against the wall that rose obtrusively between me and the students. Frustration, a sense of helplessness, and cynicism ensued. But more numerous (thankfully) were the glad occasions when students showed the spark that ignited a bit of learning, and the warmth and glow that followed dispelled doubts within.

Resolute and committed, Jesus neither lacked inner energy nor came close to burnout. He drew on limitless reserves of the Spirit's power (John 3:34). Who ever had more reason to abandon his pupils than Christ? Was there a band of disciples as querulous as the twelve? They fought among themselves for positions of prominence and prestige (Luke 9:46; 22:24). They lacked insight into the most elemental parable (Mark 4:13). After having fellowshiped with the Savior in intimate settings, they professed ignorance of the fundamental feature of His relationship with the Father (John 14:9). At the cross, they deserted. Yet Jesus consistently and compassionately remains true to these frail students; He faithfully mentors them. After Pentecost, the Paraclete will carry on that ministry.

To associate and identify with the Mentor-Teacher, we need to manifest the meekness Christ consistently displayed:

> Here is humility without hypocrisy, and the ability to endure humiliation without resentment. The meek dares to believe . . . is not afraid of missing now what God has promised at the last; will never snatch by force what must be obtained by faith, for it is faith and patience that inherit the promises. Meekness, surely, is one of the greatest adventures of all. The men to whom God ultimately entrusts the most stand out as great and blessed in meekness. . . . Meekness dares to ask but never presumes to grasp. . . . It counts on God for the culmination of His righteous purpose and casts aside as totally worthless the carnal and clumsy tools of violence. . . . I am meek says the Master.[9]

6

AWAKENING POTENTIAL

Jesus saith unto them, My meat is to do the will of him that sent me, and to finish his work.

John 4:34.

My views on motivation are best summed up in the following tale:

A fire broke out in a cramped attic. The firemen who rushed to the rescue found a man heavily asleep. They tried to carry him down the stairs but could not, and they despaired of saving him. Then the chief arrived and said: "Wake him up and he'll save himself."

The moral of the story is clear. Children bored and asleep will not be affected by a well-intentioned rescuer. They need to be awakened to their potential, and they will save themselves.[1]

Motivation is the *key* to learning. To paraphrase the proverb: "You can lead a student to learning, but you can't make him *think*!" The most sophisticated techniques, the most modern facilities and materials, the most expensive technology become useless if the student does not *want* to learn. Unless he perceives the learning experience as relevant and an integral part of his own life, teachers' efforts become futile. This is exactly the point of greatest frustration for teachers. "If only I could get him motivated to learn," they sigh in desperation.

I have scanned scores of student reports, over the years, and the disheartening words glared at me from pale pages: *apathetic, lacks initiative, unmotivated*. Teachers' despair is etched upon those folders. Students of promise, with seemingly limitless potential, never advanced beyond the elemental levels, not because they lacked ability, but because they lacked motivation. No one preoccupied with failure feels motivated; it is the most significant deterrent to success. Schools have to be places where it is *safe* to fail. To encourage students, one teacher displayed "motivating mottoes" throughout his classroom:

1. In this class, it is permissible to make mistakes.
2. An error is not a terror.
3. Goofs are lessons.
4. You may err, but don't embrace your error. Don't dwell on it, don't excuse it.
5. Mistakes are for correcting.
6. Value your correction, not your error.
7. Don't let failure go to your head.[2]

Finding the Motivation

In the scientific study of human behavior, psychologists have found motivation an intriguing concept. What causes people to behave in certain ways? Why do some people need but the slightest provocation for action, while others languish in inactivity, unmoved by cheers, jeers, or tears? Some are go-getters, others inert. Some jump the gun; others, lethargically, seem deadened by the shot. More important, how do teachers with scientific knowledge and artistic insight combine those elements that overcome inertia and generate momentum?

Motivational theorists have identified several components of the motivation process: *goals, energy, momentum,* and *incentive.* Each act of human behavior is comprised of an ensemble of these elements. In a sense, every person feels motivated. The issue is toward *what* is the person motivated? The *what* of motivation involves the identification of *goals.* Without a prior statement of goals, we talk meaninglessly about motivation. Goals are the intentions. They constitute the places we want to go—the people we want to become—the desires we want to accomplish. Motivation will remain a vague, frivolous flapping of wings in the air of indecision unless a destiny drives us. We begin at the point of our present awareness, but we must ultimately identify our terminus. A lodestone with a magnetic force must pull or propel us toward accomplishments.

Christ Jesus took a ragtag group of men and motivated them toward once unthinkable and unattainable goals. In systematic fashion, strategically employing the elements of motivation, Jesus succeeded in moving the disciples from fishnets and tax booths in Galilee to world-shaking adventures that eventually spanned the globe. As the Motivator-Teacher, He knew they must see a clear destiny before they could establish a direction.

Jesus was goal directed. He had unswervingly adhered to the goal His Father had given Him. The unaltered tempo of the imperative was in His every move. The *musts* of John's Gospel underscore that absolute, undistracted commitment to the God-given goals that ordered His life: ". . . So *must* the Son of man be lifted up" (John 3:14, *italics added*); "He *must* needs go through Samaria" (John 4:4, *italics added*); "I *must* work the works of him that sent me . . ." (John 9:4, *italics added*); ". . . He *must* rise again from the dead" (John 20:9, *italics added*).

Jesus admitted His motivation to do His Father's will: "My meat is to do the will of him that sent me . . ." (John 4:34). Over forty times in John's Gospel, the word *sent* is recorded. Jesus saw Himself as the Sent One, on a specific mission dedicated to a single task.

Too often lives become wasted through dissipation of energies. Too many things intrude, and goals become conflicting or constricting. With our limited time in this life, we cannot attempt to do everything. The people whose lives have been marked by accomplishment have limited their endeavors. They delimited and defined their goals. From numerous options, they selected ones worthy of life's labors. With calculated thought Paul the apostle did the "one thing" (Philippians 3:13). He systematically inventoried his life and divided everything into categories of gain and loss. Much like a stock-market analysis, he relegated many things to the loss column and assigned priority to only one thing— deliberately and reflectively pressing toward the goal of God. Christ never became careless in His life or in His teaching. His remarks were never "offhand," His actions never off course. He had a baptism to be baptized with, and He was straitened until it was accomplished (Luke 12:50). The intensely all-absorbing object of our Lord's life was the integrating, focal point of all His actions. Fragmented purposelessness never dissipated His efforts. The core of commitment around which He wrapped every movement of His life provided unity and accomplishment.

A single life theme has dominated few writers and activists the way it has Greece's celebrated writer Nikos Kazantzakis. Kazantzakis attributed his prodigious literary output to his acceptance of this goal: "Every integral man has inside him, in his hearts of hearts, a mystic center around which all else revolves. This mystic whirling lends unity to his thoughts and actions; it helps him find or invent the cosmic harmony. . . . Alas for the man who does not feel himself governed inside by an absolute monarch. His ungoverned, incoherent life is scattered to the four winds."[3]

When seized by the grand idea that becomes forever after the impetus for every thought and motive, a person heads toward greatness. This kind of discovery, made only (unfortunately) by a few, risk-taking people, revolutionizes outlooks and in-looks: It broadens and clarifies perspectives. Through it, identities are gained and regained. The heat it provides skims away superficialities, like dross from the smelting of gold.

Eminent cardiac specialist George Sheehan relates his own discovery, when running became the mystic center of his life:

> Then I discovered running and began the long road back. Running made me free. It rid me of concern for the opinion of others. Dispensed me from rules and regulations imposed from outside. Running let me start from scratch.
>
> It stripped off those layers of programmed activity and thinking. Developed new priorities. . . . Running changed my attitude about work and play. About whom I really liked and who really like me. Running let me see my twenty-four hour day in a new light and my life style from a different point of view, from the inside instead of out. Running was a discovery. . . .[4]

C. T. Studd, England's famed athlete and member of the fabled Cambridge seven of a century ago, who forsook fortune and notoriety to toil for Christ on several continents in missionary service, had an overpowering vision. He said: "If Jesus Christ be God and died for me, then no sacrifice can be too great for me to make for Him."

Identifying the Goal

Jesus gave the disciples a goal. Previously, they had felt content with the pedestrian world of boats and fishnets. But as important as the everyday was, it was locked into time. In Christ they discovered the sphere of service for eternity and knew, when they found it, they needed to look no farther: "Lord, to whom shall we go? thou hast the words of eternal life" (John 6:68). One goal, independent of all others, seized upon and fiercely followed, provides the source for motivation.

The Bible's pages are replete with references to people who achieved distinction because they had an all-consuming goal. Nehemiah committed himself to the rebuilding of the city of Jerusalem after the Babylonian devastation. David's unification and consolidation of Israel stands out markedly as his achievement. Likewise today's Christian must discard all other alluring options in order to accomplish anything of note for God. But we must translate the goal we undertake into measurable, temporal accomplishment. Teachers may conceive of holy quests, and be enraptured with heavenly visions, but their work must take flesh-and-blood forms. All that God does is worked out in the everyday world of harsh and heroic reality, but it must not begin there. Initially, God's goals lie beyond the commonplace; but once identified, they must take on the mortal form of daily duty. "Great services reveal our possibilities; little services reveal our consecration." Out of common clay God makes men and women.

During one phase in my life, the game of golf became a passion. I enjoyed the leisurely pastime, escaping the pressing concerns of fretful living and finding respite amid the beauties God provides on a golf course. Sweet breezes and soft clouds and velvety green carpet underfoot are pleasant surroundings for any day. My early efforts at the game, although enjoyable, were not particularly productive. Effort alone could not provide a solution to my dismal play. As I observed and analyzed successful golfers, I realized the missing ingredient in my own game: I did not lack ability or skill; I had competency enough to play the game. However, I learned I needed a sense of direction. I thought it was enough to hit the ball far and consistently. In my preoccupation with hitting, I neglected the goal of the game—getting the ball into the hole in the *fewest* number of strokes. Soon I concentrated on this objective. I reminded myself what I was up to. Hitting the ball (though necessary) was not my *final* goal: I had to do it with a minimum of strokes (fewer than my competitor, at least). When I realized this, I became a better and more relaxed golfer and mobilized my efforts more efficiently and more satisfyingly.

Several years ago, speaking to an audience of high-school, college, and career-age young people at a weekend conference, I led them through a series of exercises in motivation. First I encouraged them to identify the goals which were their *present* source of purpose. They responded to the questions:

1. What would you like to be doing five years from now?
2. What would you like to be doing one year from now?
3. Where would you like to be living five years from now?
4. Where would you like to be living one year from now?
5. What are you *presently* doing that will lead to items 1–4?

To my chagrin, I found the majority of young people had not given any serious thought to those kinds of questions. Few had attempted to identify goals, and most were not moving in any meaningful fashion toward goals. Satisfied with meandering about, letting life's stream carry them capriciously where it could, they appeared to accept drifting as their principal activity.

By the weekend's conclusion, we had achieved some success in reflecting upon important goals. Some people chose quite unrealistic goals; others felt too timid to make choices. Many found the process of goal identification painful.

A few years ago, a good friend of mine indicated that he felt discontent with his life and decided he wanted more purpose and relevance. After some discussion, we identified a few relevant and reachable goals. He expressed his sincere desire to reach those goals; I did all I could to encourage him. Weeks later, I asked him how he was doing *now* and *what* he was doing to get closer to the goals. He replied frankly: "Nothing!" Several months later, the same question brought the same answer. Years later, he had not advanced an inch! Great intentions—but inadequate motivation. Failure to initiate action that would begin the satisfying journey left him idly unable to show any accomplishment.

"What do you want to be when you grow up?" is not such a foolish question. A former student recently complained that her brother was without purpose. "He drifts aimlessly," she remarked forlornly. "Doesn't know where he wants to go. Doesn't give much thought to what he wants to be, and the sad thing is one day he'll wake up and find he's nothing. He's going nowhere, and he'll regret it." The English language holds few more regrettable words than, "If only I had. . . ."

The Lord Jesus told the fishermen He would make them "fishers of men," but they had to follow Him. In response to His summons, they forsook everything and obeyed. Christ sets worthy goals before us, but to reach them, we must free ourselves from all other obligations and options. No strings attached! Let the dead bury their dead. Paul told his pupil Timothy that a good soldier does not entangle himself with the affairs of this world, so he may please the one who chose and recruited him for service (2 Timothy 2:4). The spider's web of excessive entanglements traps the fly of good intentions and seals its doom. Procrastination is perilous! We must firmly establish and faithfully follow our plans. Preoccupation with peripheral concerns will surely sidetrack the best of us. Jesus set His face like a flint (Isaiah 50:7). For the disciples who would follow Him, He planned lessons well in advance. One education axiom says, "All learning begins with goals." Motivation not moored to objectives drifts into capriciousness.

Providing Incentives

Goals must have incentives aligned with them. The motivator-teacher knows that direction detached from satisfaction will eventually degenerate into apathy. The trek toward the target, begun with exhilaration, becomes a fatiguing foot dragging when a student feels no sense of significance in the goals. Offering incentives at the outset and providing them at the completion motivates. Jesus promised success at the end of the excursion. He never minimized the severity of the ordeal, but He assured the willing ones that the enterprise would prove worth their while. Whatever calls for self-investment can only make that claim when there is sufficient inducement. We seldom follow a call for sacrifice and submission unless we envision a reward commensurate with the cost.

Young children, particularly, need tangible incentives to motivate them. As parents (as well as teachers), my wife and I regularly provided our children with incentives for successful schoolwork. We knew they had to have something to work for. We gave worthwhile rewards for a finished task, and over time we tried to have our children realize that successful accomplishment is its own reward. To enhance motivation, a teacher needs a system of incentives.

God appointed Elisha to succeed the prophet Elijah. When the time for Elijah's departure arrived, Elisha made one request of him: "a double portion of thy spirit be upon me" (2 Kings 2:9). Elijah's response placed demands upon Elisha. "If you see me when I go," said Elijah, "then you will have your request." Elijah began his journey to the appointed place of his ascent into heaven. Repeatedly wherever they paused, Elijah had told Elisha to remain, but insistent, Elisha had contended he would not separate himself from the prophet. The condition for the blessing depended upon Elisha's physical presence at Elijah's departure. Firmly, resolutely, in anticipation of the promise (incentive), Elisha persisted toward the mark and with his own eyes beheld the spectacle of Elijah's departure (2 Kings 2:11, 12). God held out too appealing an incentive for him to dismiss it. Elisha refused to be deterred from his goal and the prospect of spiritual power: a double portion of Elijah's spirit was worth the scorn of the sons of the prophets and the rebukes of Elijah himself.

With masterly motivation Jesus provided strong incentives for His disciples, which those who grasped for them refused to renounce, despite the difficulties involved in reaching the ultimate goal. Self-investment and identity, *major* aspects of motivation, elicit commitment from followers. Whenever the goal offered to us involves something vital to our identities, we become more likely to pursue it. If we see tasks and efforts as extensions of our beings, we will invest ourselves with greater industry. Perception has a critical role in motivation. Jacob, with keener perception than Esau, saw the value of the birthright and the blessing (Genesis 25:33; 27:27, 28). Esau, with dulled sensitivities, could not see beyond the moment or appreciate anything beyond his immediate appetite. However, Jacob estimated the eventual worth of an aspiration and the act. The fulfillment of priestly prerogatives of the birthright meant blessing to and prosperity through his progeny. The transformation of Jacob's character, begun at Bethel, blossomed at Peniel, and his name change reflected the character change (Genesis 28:13–15; 32:28).

Our Lord motivated His disciples by promising fulfillment of identities and abilities. Christ holds the prospect of "self-actualization" by providing "self-transcendence." We all would like to fulfill ourselves. We would like to become all God intended us to be. Within each of us lies the unspoken but penetrating perception of the person we would like to become—the mature person in Christ (Ephesians 4:13). We imagine ourselves spiritually dynamic and creatively Christian, but we also recognize that an image that confines and presses us into stunted molds constrains us. We feel unable to break the shackles and unfetter ourselves from these disfiguring identities, and we wish we were all Prometheus *un*bound.

Abraham Maslow incorrectly says that we can actualize ourselves by ourselves, and he is equally wrong when he tells us we should make self-actualization the goal of our lives. Victor Frankl comes closer to the truth when he wisely cautions against self-absorption. Something must beckon us, or else all victories will be Pyrrhic and all conquests self-defeats. Frankl, who learned his lesson in a concentration camp, has earned the right to teach us:

Self-actualization is a good thing; however, I maintain that man can only actualize himself to the extent to which he fulfills meaning. Then self-actualization occurs spontaneously; it is contravened when it is made an end in itself. . . . Man . . . finds identity to the extent to which he commits himself to something beyond himself, to a cause greater than himself. . . . Existence falters unless it is lived in terms of transcendence toward something beyond itself.[5]

Clarifying Identity

As the Motivator-Teacher, the first and fundamental act of our Lord was to alert His followers to the meaning of life. He linked all subsequent adventure and action to the permanence of God's eternal mission. As learners devote themselves to that which is beyond them, they increasingly actualize that within them. When we march to the rhythm of our own monotonous and deafening beat, we soon find ourselves in a parade of one, shuffling through blind alleys that lead only to dead-end streets. When identity and eternity converge, things, providential and personal, develop. As God breathed His own breath into Abram and transformed him into Abraham, as Christ held out to Simon the prospect for accomplishment in the renamed Peter, as the self-willed Saul of Tarsus was made into the pliable apostle Paul—so the new names we are given reflect the realization of our "selves." Names indicate character, and each name change establishes new perceptions and prospects and redefines and clarifies once fuzzy and weak identities.

Teachers see students in terms of what they can *become* and hold out to them identities into which they can develop. Our Lord was interested in names, but not in labels. The Motivator-Teacher denounced rigid categories and classifications that preclude change and development. Her countrymen may continue to refer to her as "Rahab the harlot," but God saved and transformed her, freeing her from this stigma (Joshua 6:17, 25). Her new identity would make its way into the Savior's genealogy (Matthew 1:5).

Avoiding Apathy

Jesus had a genius for taking the most unworkable material and imbuing it with spirit and zest. Of all the sins in education, the most heinous, perhaps, is apathy. The disinterested, I-don't-care attitude is abominable. Boredom rules the kingdom of this educational age: Students today continually complain of it. Sometimes Christ's followers today seem to suffer from *ennui*—the chronic apathy that paralyzes the will and atrophies the spirit. Partly this results from the lack of connection between Christ's call and personal identity. The word *identity* comes from the Latin word for "same." Logically, therefore, identity comes from associations. As believer-students unite with Christ, their identities develop.

Apathy and motivation are antithetical. A bored believer cannot feel motivated. Levi sat at the "seat of custom," performing the conventional and routine activities, complacently engaged in another day's duties. Jesus walked by, summoned him to service, and changed Levi. From working exclusively in Caesar's government, he was enlisted in the service of the King of kings (Matthew 9:9).

During my teaching days in public school, I often gave nicknames to students. These playful identities, reflective of some characteristic or mild idiosyncrasy, I never intended to be derogatory. The students generally liked the appellations and accepted them with fondness. One boy, quick in his actions and shorter than the others, often became the butt of their jokes. I nicknamed him *Scooter*. Whenever we had recess or gym class, I would organize various games and divide the students into teams. Scooter began to take an increased interest in these activities. Previously listless and only marginally involved, soon after the students called him Scooter, he became a celebrity of sorts. The games that required speed and quickness would invariably find him on the winning team. His whole demeanor changed over the course of the year, and his status was elevated. Eventually, he achieved more and gained social acceptance.

As the great Motivator, Christ brings out the best in us. He sees below the deceptive exteriors that obscure potential, and He probes until He touches the part of us around which a rich identity can grow. By His grace, He permits previously untapped possibilities to spring forth and flourish.

Fulfilling Needs

One fertile area of motivational research relates behavior to need fulfillment. Much of our behavior we can explain in terms of our attempts to satisfy needs, and researchers have sought to identify and explain our common needs. Some fairly simplistic and superficial explanations suggest we can reduce all motivation to curiosity or restoration of an inner equilibrium. However, more critical needs motivate us toward significant goals.

In preparing instruction, a perceptive teacher seeks to meet the needs of learners and programs classroom experiences accordingly. Certain needs cannot be met in schools, and the teacher must exercise discretion in choosing proper goals. Leaving behind those needs others may care for or referring the student to those who will better care for them, he or she focuses on the ones the school can best deal with. The instructor who neglects the critical needs of students will reap the consequences of impaired learning and decreased motivation in students.

Physical Needs

At the basic level of human existence, survival and species propagation needs are paramount. In common with all life, humans cannot survive without minimal satisfaction of physiological needs. The Motivator-Teacher assures His disciples of adequate provision. The heavenly Father, who feeds sparrows and provides homes for swallows, attends to our survival needs: "Your heavenly Father feedeth them. Are ye not much better than they?" (Matthew 6:26). On more than one occasion, I have provided resources for students, assisting children from deprived homes, who lacked essentials—food, clothing, and funds for school activities. Students suffering lacks in these areas are not motivated to learn. Good teachers become alert to needs and find ways to meet them. Even the best teacher cannot reach a child who hasn't eaten properly (and I have come across a number of them). Unfilled stomachs require attention before unfilled minds.

Charlie sat listlessly in class, seldom attentive to the task at hand, never, as contemporary educators would say, "on task." His mind always seemed somewhere else—chasing his stomach, I suppose. He never prepared homework assignments and constantly daydreamed. A health referral disclosed that he suffered from a systemic infection. Inadequate medical and dental care had resulted in disease and infection. Until we cared for his basic medical needs, it was useless to try to motivate him to higher learning levels, to more "cognitive complexity."

Emotional Needs

Love, self-acceptance, and worthwhile relationships manifest themselves at higher levels on the needs hierarchy. William Glasser identifies love and worth as the most pressing needs at this level.[6] Psychologist Lawrence Crabb labels them "security and significance."[7] Each of us needs to feel loved; it is the fundamental desire of all humans and a powerful motivator. Loveless classes shrivel the souls and minds of learners. Leo Buscaglia, humanist-educator, attracts a wide following and large readership. Often, with despairing audiences, he simply shares the message of his popular book Love.[8]

Some students sit in classes unmoved and seemingly unmovable, refusing to engage in schoolwork of any kind. Rewards and tangible incentives prove useless. Indifferent to all entreaties, with heavy defiance they resist any inducement to learn. Some continue on to the end of their school careers in this sad and stagnant state; others become statistics on the dropout charts.

Jean Mizer, in her compellingly compassionate short story, "Cipher in the Snow," portrays a young boy who, denied love and affection by family and friends, plodded along against the ugly indifference. A phantom to himself, ignored by teachers and classmates, distant from life, he crept within himself and disappeared. One day he disembarked from a schoolbus and died:

At school, the giggling, shuffling morning noise quieted as the news went down the halls. I passed a huddle of girls. "Who was it? Who dropped dead on the way to school?" I heard one of them half-whisper.

"Don't know his name; some kid from Milford Corners," was the reply.

It was like that in the faculty room and the principal's office . . . "I didn't know the boy," the principal admitted levelly, "and in last year's sophomore personalities column, I noted that you were listed as his favorite teacher."

I drove through the snow and down the bad canyon road to the Evans place and thought about the boy, Cliff Evans. His favorite teacher! I thought. He hasn't spoken two words to me in two years! I could see him in my mind's eye all right, sitting back there in the last seat in my . . . class. He came in the room by himself and left by himself. "Cliff Evans," I muttered to myself, "a boy who never talked." I thought a minute. "A boy who never smiled. I never saw him smile once."

. . . A little boy kept walking after me, a little boy with a peaked, pale face; a skinny body in faded jeans; and big eyes that had looked and searched for a long time and then had become veiled.

I could guess how many times he'd been chosen last to play sides in a game, how many whispered child conversations had excluded him, how many times he hadn't been asked. I could see and hear the faces and voices that said over and over, "You're dumb. You're dumb. You're a nothing, Cliff Evans."

We couldn't find ten students in the school who had known Cliff Evans well enough to attend the funeral as his friends. . . . I attended the services with them and sat through it with a lump of cold lead in my chest and a big resolve growing through me.

I have never forgotten Cliff Evans nor that resolve. He has been my challenge year after year, class after class. I look up and down the rows carefully each September at the unfamiliar faces. I look for veiled eyes or bodies scrouged into a seat in an alien world. "Look kids," I say silently, "I may not do anything else for you this year, but not one of you is going to come out of here a nobody. I'll work or fight to the bitter end . . . but I won't have one of you coming out of here thinking himself a zero. . . ."[9]

Each of us has an insistent need to see life as meaningful and worthwhile. Tragically, in our schools, so many move, without motivation or meaning, through a numbed existence, never knowing a sense of self-worth. William Glasser identifies the consequences of a life devoid of love and worth: pain! Without minimum satisfaction of these divinely endowed needs, we soon experience emptiness. Pain settles in, and we cannot indefinitely endure prolonged pain. We seek to escape or reduce the agony and may consider any option that offers relief. Pain of soul and self, like pain of body, cannot be ignored. If it persists without relief, one forgets the unfulfilled need that prompted the pain and directs all efforts toward alleviating the pain itself.

Glasser suggests four options that become appealing. Irritability and anger cause some people to strike out against the world that provided no remedy. In the extreme, this takes the form of violent antisocial behavior that, before long, forces society to take heed and acknowledge the need. Others take the appealing recourse of emotional preoccupation. Typically in today's impersonal world, depression has become an attractive option, because it provides a buffer for the loss of esteem and lack of love; depression is often linked to suicide. When life offers no security or significance, as an increasingly large number of people have found, suicide becomes potently appealing. In severe cases flights into fantasy worlds may occur, and retreat into a painless world of delusions finds its takers. In the fourth and most respectable and legitimate option, symptoms develop that may require a medical solution. The waiting rooms of physicians are crowded beyond capacity in this overmedicated society where the kind word and tender touch of the doctor seem more acceptable than the psychiatrist's couch.[10]

Jesus is the need fulfiller; He is at hand. He provides physical and material needs: ". . . I have not seen the righteous forsaken, nor his seed begging bread," David asserted (Psalms 37:25). "I have loved thee with an everlasting love. . . ." Jeremiah knew from experience (Jeremiah 31:3). Jesus gives us dignity and worth, despite B. F. Skinner's claims to the contrary.[11]

Readiness Timing

As the Motivator-Teacher, Christ always suits the experience to the level of development and the nature of the need. He attunes Himself to the "teachable moment," the time when developmentally ready learners profit most from such experiences. Jesus permits nothing in the lives of His students until they have matured in God's purposes. The concept of "readiness" is a forceful one in education. Infants crawl before they walk. Premature involvement can damage learners. Jesus did not load everything on His disciples, but waited until the opportune time to teach new lessons: "I have yet many things to say unto you, but ye cannot bear them now" (John 16:12). Paul makes a similar point, declaring that his hearers "are dull of hearing" (Hebrew 5:11) and unready for the more mature teaching.

The preadolescent and early adolescent years require sensitivity and astuteness from teachers planning appropriate experiences, for during this time, students' minds and bodies change rapidly. I have observed school programs that unwisely prescribed activities for which teenagers were unprepared. Physical education classes became embarrassing places when fundamental principles of growth and development went unheeded. Heightened body changes and peer approval, during this developmental stage, mean schools must avoid awkward expectations. Jean Jacques Rousseau, who said some silly things about education, was, nevertheless, on track when he advised: "Be content to show him things at the right moment."[12] Meaningful experiences require relevance. When education impinges on living that is partly conditioned by development, it has fueled the explosive potential for significant learning. Philip Phoenix, noted educator, strives for relevance in motivating his own students:

> Another goal in my teaching is the student's growth in personal meaning. No student is likely to learn well anything that has no significance to him as a person. I do not imply in this regard a criterion of immediate practical utility or obvious applicability to current social problems. I am simply underlining what should be pedagogic commonplace—namely, that teaching consists in making vital some portion . . . by exhibiting its intimate bearing on the life and destiny of the student.[13]

Motivation does not necessarily involve walking the easy road. Jesus refused to sacrifice significant future goals for the expediency of the immediate safe route. Rewards abound for God's people, but they do not preclude endurance and commitment. God holds out to us the prospect of eternal glory, but we first suffer a while (1 Peter 5:10). Motivator-teachers do not compromise the quality goals before them for the ephemeral, less challenging conveniences of the present hour. Not making the present needlessly tedious and unappetizing, yet they remember that maturity involves suspension of at-hand indulgences for the promised assurance of future reward. The Motivator-Teacher in His final appeal to the church calls for accomplishment and endurance, which are inseparably connected (Revelation 2:11, 17, 26; 3:5, 12, 21).

7
STANDING BETWEEN

For there is one God, and one mediator between God and men, the man Christ Jesus.

1 Timothy 2:5

And I, if I be lifted up from the earth, will draw all men unto me.

John 12:32

Somebody once asked, ''and what does Jesus Christ stand for?'' The answer he received was unexpected. ''He doesn't stand for anything, He stands between.''[1]

It is one of the ways of God in all His workings to grant His blessings through an intermediary. . . . Without the mediating element all is lost. . . . But to me it seems that through every sphere of God's activity runs the great principle of mediation; and to me the presence of Christ is like the air, making available for my need the love of God. . . . Christ is the mediator . . . He stands—the vital breath—'twixt God and us.[2]

Rarely do we find anyone so willing to put his life on the line that he becomes the line! Though we all have convictions and may declare allegiance to a cause, it is another thing to be the *very* cause itself. Christ Jesus became *the* Cause. Ultimately everything centers, not in the plan or purpose, but in *the* Person. Influential personalities throughout history became dominant because they were inseparable from the cause they championed and the ideology they espoused. The charismatic teachers who coalesced within themselves the doctrines and teachings associated with their ideas have transformed societies and have left legacies. But the effective teacher must stand between the students who surround him and the world that would assault them.

Teachers as Mediators

To be meaningful, education must be mediated. Teachers are the go-betweens. Unless the teacher transmutes them into tangible events, the experiences of the curriculum will simply remain lifeless irrelevancies. Education includes both transmission and transmutation. Teachers have always been mediators to their students. Even the most passive teacher impacts and shapes the classroom experiences. Some people naively expect a teacher to be a neutral commodity, but research has shown that even laissez-faire-style teachers, whose presence seems of little consequence, serve as filters, distilling and distorting learning.[3] Marshall McLuhan's imaginative interpretation of media attests to the force with which mediation impacts messages.[4] Lessons, mediated through the person of the teacher, undergo modification, and not all teachers equally or equitably transmit education. Teachers are not inert conduits, like tubes, which transport water to faucets, without affecting the taste. All education the student assimilates has acquired the character of the teacher. Tendencies and tastes, preferences and proclivities become elements in that education. Students do not simply learn subjects and skills. Sometimes in subtle ways, building up over time, a part of the teacher accretes within the student.

I can see within myself, in mannerisms and methods, touches and traces of teachers I have had. At times, I find myself pausing during a classroom lesson and smiling curiously at the uncanny resemblance between my words or actions and those of a teacher from my past who gave them to me. Sometimes a particularly dramatic resemblance makes me feel as if a specter from that haunting past had pervaded the room. Vocal inflections, whimsical gestures, style of presentation are not merely imitations but expressions of something internalized that, quite spontaneously and unforced, shows itselves in the classroom. Those teachers from that impressionable past continue their performances within their pedagogical progeny.

Teaching is a performance. All teachers are artists in part. A sculptor kneads the clay and shapes, with skilled and dextrous fingers, the amorphous glob into a work of art that previously existed only within his own imagination. Typically we refer to material with which an artist works as the "medium," but more accurately, the *artist* is the medium. Through him ideals are mediated, and the substance of the reality he shapes or paints or performs represents those images. Creation, itself, requires mediation. Teachers, in their critical and creative task, transform immature learners into mature students by taking the goals of education and implementing programs that will, in turn, become realized in the students' lives. But to do this, teachers mentally and imaginatively reconstruct within themselves and then seek to reproduce that within students. If education is different from or less than that creative process, then teaching is reduced to technique and requires only the simple services of automatons.

Christ the Mediator

Jesus Christ, God's ordained Mediator, alone spans the immense gulf between God and man. The yawning, seemingly unbridgeable chasm, mocking mankind in his helplessness and separating him from God, has finally seen the One who can touch both sides of the crevasse. In American folklore, the famed Paul Bunyan, with gargantuan strides, could traverse the most terrifying and hostile terrain. He could step across canyons as easily and as quickly as we can climb the stairs. God's great Reconciler of men (2 Corinthians 5:18, 19), suspended between earth and heaven on the cross, in that single act of obedient sacrifice (Romans 5:19) joined man to God.

During the divisive days of social upheaval in America, a little girl gained notoriety by displaying a sign at a political rally. On the placard were written these words: BRING US TOGETHER. Job lamented the lack of someone who could come and lay hands upon him and God and bring them together. But now the "daysman" of Job's desire has come, and the haunting alienation that seemed forever to want a solution has found its satisfaction and fulfillment in the incarnate God (Job 9:33). Little wonder that Paul exclaimed: ". . . Great is the mystery of godliness: God was manifest in the flesh . . ." (1 Timothy 3:16). Until the Teacher-Mediator came, no one else could represent God to man and thereby represent man to God. The closest approximations in the Old Testament were the prophet and the priest. The prophets of old, beginning perhaps with Enoch (Jude 14), spoke for God. Duly ordained, the prophets proclaimed the basis on which God could and would meet with mankind. Finally, in the "fullness of time," the Lord Jesus Christ came as a prophet along the lines of Moses: "The Lord thy God will raise up unto thee a Prophet from the midst of thee, of thy brethren, like unto me; unto him ye shall hearken" (Deuteronomy 18:15).

Moses the Mediator

Moses was the mediator for the children of Israel. In response to the voice of God calling out of the burning bush, Moses accepted this commission to mediate between the children of Israel and Pharaoh of Egypt (Exodus 3:2–10). Initially reluctant, Moses then complied and became Jehovah's representative to the enslaved sons of Jacob. Throughout his lifetime, Moses remained the one through whom God communicated to Israel. Of him the Bible says: "And there arose not a prophet since in Israel like unto Moses, whom the Lord knew face to face" (Deuteronomy 34:10). In the life of Christ, Moses (along with Elijah) was privy to plans concerning ". . . his decease [Greek: *exodus*] which he should accomplish at Jerusalem" (Luke 9:31).

Whenever a problem arose within Israel's camp Moses invariably would mediate. Aaron, as High Priest, often acted as Moses' spokesman, but God transmitted the message first to Moses. Indeed, it is unlikely that God intended to separate the two offices of mediator and High Priest, but He deferred to Moses' apprehension and allowed Aaron to accompany him and assume that special role.[5] When Israel desecrated itself before the golden calf, Moses pleaded with God to withhold judgment and offered to substitute himself: "Yet now, if thou wilt forgive their sin—; and if not, blot me, I pray thee, out of thy book which thou hast written" (Exodus 32:32). During forty wearisome years of wilderness wanderings, Moses received God's instruction at the mercy seat in the Tabernacle and represented God to the nation (Exodus 25:21, 22).

As highly esteemed as Moses was, yet his mediatorship was limited to the Law. By contrast, ". . . grace and truth came by Jesus Christ" (John 1:17). The Mediator-Teacher far surpasses the office of Moses, and His provision of saving grace eclipses the condemnation of the Law. Unlike the tabernacle of old, which housed tablets of stone with words of judgment written on them, this One who tabernacled among us was ". . . full of grace and truth" (John 1:14).

Who Can Mediate?

I have often wondered, as I have pondered the origin of evil, why Lucifer thought he could successfully usurp the place of the

Son of God (Isaiah 14:12–14). The privileged angel, who enjoyed a place of intimacy and a position of elevation in the hierarchy of heaven, deliberately challenged the supremacy of God's Son and sought for himself the coveted title of Morning Star. Was this maniacal maneuver prompted by Satan's presumption that God would be unable to do anything about it without violating His own character? Satan, I believe, must have thought God incapable of avenging that heinous offense and at the same time reconciling the world to Himself in one single act of love and justice. Satan knew something vital about the character of God; after all, he had enjoyed and observed God's every movement in that timeless realm before creation. Satan knew that God was One (James 2:19). He also knew that a mediator was between two: "Now a mediator is not a mediator of one . . ." (Galatians 3:20). Who could possibly combine the qualities that would serve to satisfy both God's justice and God's love? Angels could not be mediators. But a man could! Little did Satan suspect that God would create man in His own image (Genesis 1:26). God would provide a mediator in a man—in *the* Man: "But this man, after he had offered one sacrifice for sins for ever, sat down on the right hand of God" (Hebrews 10:12). This is the strong Man whom God had promised He would send: "Let thy hand be upon the man of thy right hand, upon the son of man whom thou madest strong for thyself" (Psalms 80:17). Hence the reason for Paul's ecstatic ejaculation: ". . . Great is the mystery of godliness: God was manifest in the flesh . . ." (1 Timothy 3:16). God would, Himself, in the person of His Son, become man. So in Christ Jesus we have both God and Man. I personally prefer to avoid the term *God-Man*. To me it smacks of a *tertium quid*—a third kind of something or other. In one person, two natures (hypostatically joined) in perfect symmetry, unity, and proportion combine without conflict or confusion.

The Lord Jesus alone could make His way into the lives of men and women and meet continuously with God's unqualified favor. Here is perfect manhood, perfect humanity as God intended. This One can make the unrivaled claim to being the Mediator-Teacher.

Teachers as Advocates

Often students find schools lonely places. Sometimes the impersonality of modern institutions frightens children, and they spend fearful and friendless days in places supposed to be supportive and caring. What an encouragement to such a child to find a teacher who senses his apprehension and comes alongside to help. How necessary in such circumstances to have *advocates*. The reassuring smile, the gentle hand on the shoulder, the kind word—little things that cost nothing but make the difference between delight and despair, between victory and defeat.

In addition to the three *R*s of education, there is the fourth, critical *R* of relationships. No significant learning can occur apart from meaningful relationships in, as Martin Buber phrased it, "I-thou" encounters.[6] Relationships within schools range along a continuum, from the supportive to the hostile. Chronic confrontative postures in which teachers and students continually lock horns in battle is not the scholar's stance. I have taught in schools where antagonism tore the relationships to shreds. Wounded egos and battered pride shuffled limply and purposelessly, casualties of the war-weary atmosphere. The daily dread of being on the firing line, with no back-up troops, soon leads to battle fatigue and teacher burnout.[7] Antagonism mounts without reprieve, and soon hostilities take their toll; although some people may wave white flags, few problems ever get solved. Adversarial relationships destroy worthwhile learning. Education cannot survive, much less thrive, in this kind of climate.

If a teacher fails to take up a student's rightful cause, put his arm around him lovingly, and point him to the possibilities in his life, someone else may come along who offers a less acceptable alternative. When the militant social activist Malcom X was a student, one English teacher, Mr. Ostrowski, made Malcom feel he liked him. Malcom looked up to Mr. Ostrowski and sought his advice on a number of issues. One day Malcom remarked that he wanted to become a lawyer. As Malcom X recalls the incident:

Mr. Ostrowski looked surprised, I remember and leaned back in his chair and clasped his hands behind his head. He kind of half-smiled and said, "Malcom one of life's first needs is for us to be realistic. Don't misunderstand me now. We all here like you, you know that. But you've got to be realistic about being a nigger. A lawyer—that's no realistic goal for a nigger. You need to think about something you *can* be."[8]

Malcom's future life took shape right there. At that point, he confessed, he began to change. Something within him—inside—underwent a transformation, and anger and venom began to build and flow. He had been raised in a Christian home, but his religious life changed, and he became a Moslem. His voice was heard—the strident, defiant, revolutionary voice—during the next decades. If Mr. Ostrowski had acted as a mediator, what a difference it could have made in this influential life. Had that English teacher been that young man's advocate, the course of social history during the violent decade of the 1960s might have had a happier account. Teachers dare not minimize their influence upon students. They need to be alert to the student tottering on the brink of social aggression, the one trying to balance the fragile feelings about himself and the hostile world he perceives. Malcom X evaluates that critical time in his life: "Whatever I have done since then, I have driven myself to become a success at it. I've often thought that if Mr. Ostrowski had encouraged me to become a lawyer, I would today probably be among the city's black bourgeoisie."[9]

Our Advocate With the Father

Into this strife-ridden world, the Mediator-Teacher came to stand against the forces of destruction and between His followers and the archenemy of their souls. The elder John tenderly alerts us to our Advocate: ". . . We have an advocate with the Father, Jesus Christ the righteous" (1 John 2:1). A classroom should be quite unlike a law court, but sometimes similarities exist. Courts are structured along adversarial lines, and conflicts generate the momentum for the contest between the litigants. Presumably, in the classroom, teachers commit themselves, with students, to a mutually beneficial goal. Each willingly cooperates in the effort, and fusion not fission generates the momentum.

Satan, the "accuser of our brethren," always stands against us (Revelation 12:9, 10). The devil, "your adversary" (1 Peter 5:8), purposes to generate conflict that will debilitate and destroy all our efforts. He creates chasms and chaos. The avowed enemy of God's eternal purpose, he has sworn to wreak havoc wherever possible. He divides and drives wedges into relationships, disrupting, where he can, by disharmony and strife. He seeks strategic openings and begins a campaign of assault on our souls.

As our Mediator the Lord Jesus takes the advocate's place beside us. He comes alongside, as the Greek word for "advocate" implies: *paraklesis*. He is the *paraclete* who shadows us with His presence; He is the advocate who never abandons us. Satan had divine permission to penetrate the hedges that protected Job. Without permission, the devil could not have afflicted that righteous man in any way. Satan moves in all the areas of Job's saintly life. Stealthily, he invades them one by one, soon reducing Job to a desolate figure, stripped of his dignity, but never violating his integrity. God guarded the bastion of his soul and would not allow the adversary to tamper with that inviolable core (Job 2:3).

Peter was a prime object of Satan's attacks. He wanted to "sift him like wheat." The Advocate would not permit it (Luke 22:31, 32). It was not the time for Peter to be tested and screened through the sieve of Satan's pressure. Advocacy takes our part in the struggle. Advocacy means He aids and abets us when the odds are stacked against us. Christ will not let the adversary get his advantage (2 Corinthians 2:11). God will not leave us open and vulnerable when our untempered souls cannot stand the strain or the straining. No temptation will overtake us unless or until we are able to bear it (1 Corinthians 10:13).

The disciples were always aware that Jesus stood between

them and the threat. When the storm beat upon their boat and threatened to capsize their cause, Jesus arose and stood between them and the assault of the sea, whipped into its frenzy by Satan's anger (Mark 4:39). That fateful night in Gethsemane's garden, when the Judas-led mob attacked the disciple band, Christ stood His ground: ". . . When the enemy shall come in like a flood, the Spirit of the Lord shall lift up a standard against him" (Isaiah 59:19). The Lord Jesus asked that vengeful mob whom they sought. When they responded, "Jesus of Nazareth," He uttered the sublime name by which God had revealed Himself to Moses (Exodus 3:14) and that had remained inexpressible by the most pious of Jews: "I AM." When confronted with the very presence of deity, they "went backward, and fell to the ground," paralyzed with fear and prostrate (although unknowingly) before incomparable majesty (John 18:1–6). ". . . If therefore ye seek me," Jesus continued, "let these go their way" (John 18:8). No one can touch those whom Christ protects. Whether the enemy seeks to intimidate or assault us, our Advocate will not capitulate. Martin Luther must have had this Gethsemane scene in mind, when, before his accusers, he declared: "Here I stand; I can do no otherwise. God help me. Amen."

An Advocate for Students

During my term of service as a guidance counselor in several schools, I chose to define my role in relational terms. I refused to function merely as a bookkeeper—quasi-administrator–test giver–record keeper. Often, I thought my colleagues debased their calling by engaging in the tedium the bureaucracy callously inflicted upon them. It required some resilience to oppose these daily intrusions, but I had been educated and trained to relate to people and guide them in their personal and academic development. The temptation to become preoccupied with paperwork, I confess, mildly enticed me, because it would free me from the much more difficult and energy-draining activities involved in helping people. Tensions within me and turmoil with administrators were part of the price I would pay for that decision.

I saw myself as an advocate for students and determined I would represent their interests, regardless of the problem or perplexity. I would not be a disciplinarian and dole out punishment; I would not become a moralizer, pronouncing curses upon them; I would not turn into a policeman, reporting their derelictions to the authorities. Instead I would listen, empathize, and seek to help them find solutions. I would stand alongside them and take their part. I may not always have agreed with them or with what they did and I could not uncritically accept their irresponsible behavior. When my values clashed with theirs, I let them know it. I did not condone irresponsibility or immorality. However, I did seek to listen sympathetically and try to help them sort out the convolutions of thoughts and feelings. I let them know that I would, in any way possible, help and assist them.

Our Lord Jesus advocates for us in this way. As His disciples, He will never allow or countenance our continuation in inexcusable and intolerable behavior. However, by virtue of the redemption we have through Him, He does give us *unqualified* acceptance. We have been made "accepted in the beloved" (Ephesians 1:6). Advocacy brings acceptance. In all the hierarchies of human needs students of psychology have developed, including that of Abraham Maslow, uncritical acceptance is critically important.[10] A hymn of sweet assurance expresses that gracious acceptance.

> *In the beloved, God's marvellous grace*
> *Calls me to dwell in this wonderful place.*
> *God sees my Savior and then He sees me,*
> *in the Beloved, accepted and free.*[11]

The Authentic Advocate

Advocacy provides unqualified acceptance and undiminished assurance of the *person*. Of all the disciples, Jesus lost none except the son of perdition, and Judas chose to place himself outside the ken of security (John 17:12). Predicating His acceptance upon personal authenticity, our Lord was the truly authentic teacher. Totally transparent in His dealings, no hint of deception or veil kept His true nature from others. He never resorted to legerdemain to impress audiences or curry favor with the crowds. Ingenuous, unsecretive, He could look His accusers in the eye and demand: "Which of you convinceth me of sin? . . ." (John 8:46).

Human teachers are incapable of such constitutional authenticity. Marred and despoiled by the corrosive effects of transgression, we can never aspire to such boldness about ourselves. Nevertheless, in a real, though relative sense, we can be authentic. The teacher unafraid to disclose himself, the authentic self, will eventually elicit response from students. Sidney Jourard hits the nail on the head, with his description of *in*authenticity:

> Much learning . . . occurs informally when students identify with the attitudes and practices displayed by their teachers. If these teachers are impersonal and have an air of perfection and imperturbability about them, the students are likely to pursue this impossible pinnacle of human performance. If a teacher has a "classroom manner" similar to her bedside manner, then it is difficult to see how the student can ever come to care about her own real self. . . . One evaluates his real self in a manner that significant others evaluate it. If one's teachers are impersonal in their transactions to students, likely the students will be impersonal in their attitude toward themselves. . . . As the teachers are, so will the students become. . . .[12]

A dearth of "realness" fills many schools. The paucity of transparency among teachers magnifies the courageous few willing to risk authenticity. Like Oliver Cromwell, these few have their portraits painted "warts and all." Teachers, as mediators of education, are also mirrors into which students look intently and in which, sadly, they often see distorted images. Teachers as mediators and mirrors both reflect and project images to students. They not only tell their students what they are, but what they can become. These teacher–looking glasses prophesy about possibilities.

The Advocate's Influence

Robert Rosenthal's research regarding teachers' expectations for students suggests that students will begin to interpret themselves in terms of teachers' expectations. What Rosenthal has termed the "Pygmalion Effect" tells us that teachers also mediate potential.[13] In ancient myth the sculptor Pygmalion created a beautiful statue and fell in love with it. Motivated by love, he behaved toward the statue as though it were actually alive, and the goddess Venus, in honor of his devotion, brought the statue to life. Translated into the celebrated stage play by George Bernard Shaw, *Pygmalion* was later adapted into the Broadway musical, *My Fair Lady*. In that show the candid remark by Eliza sums up the essence of Rosenthal's studies surrounding this phenomenon: "You see, really and truly . . . the difference between a lady and a flower girl is not how she behaves, but how she's treated. I shall always be a flower girl to Professor Higgins, because he . . . treats me as a flower girl . . . but I know I can be a lady to you because you always treat me as a lady, and always will."[14]

When teachers communicate lofty yet attainable expectations to students, they seek to adopt and aspire to those goals. One student remembers her teacher because he did just that for his students:

> Mr. Jacobs won our hearts, because he treated us as though we were already what we could only hope to become. Through his eyes, we saw ourselves as capable and decent and destined for greatness. He gave direction to our longings and left us with the conviction that our fate can be forged by our hopes and deeds; that our lives need not be shaped by accident; that our happiness does not depend upon happenstance. Mr. Jacobs introduced us to ourselves.[15]

But before those aspirations can germinate and flourish, the teacher, as an authentic advocate, must first internalize the qualities of transparency and then mediate them to students:

> And let us look at the good teacher. Probably he can be seen, without too much strain, as a rehabilitated ignoramus. He has known the hellish smugness of the cliche, the quick answer, the unchallenged certitude; he has known the awe of mystery, and the dread of the unknown—and the adventure of the life of endless inquiry. Since his pupils are presently unenlightened, he knows how to reach them. But they are not likely to accept the invitation to a life of inquiry unless by his very being as a man, the teacher is revealed as a man who has courage and who finds satisfaction and meaning . . . in his life.[16]

Christ Our Mediator

Christ as the Mediator-Teacher holds within His hand and within His Word the mirror into which we look. It not only reflects a face that needs attention (James 1:23–25), but reveals vistas that are opening and available to us as we are "changed into the same image from glory to glory" (2 Corinthians 3:18). The Son of God mediates to man all that God is; therefore, preoccupation with Him cultivates the likeness of God within us. I have often thought that when we arrive in heaven and see the Savior face-to-face, we will be amazed at how much we resemble Him. The similarity may shock us. At one level, this similarity will be the result of His grace, which has worked itself out in us; and we shall be like Him, for ". . . we shall see him as he is" (1 John 3:2). However, at another level of experience, I believe the similarity will result from our contemplation of Him. As we look longingly into the reflective face of Christ, we find ourselves fashioned by His countenance. As we let the glory of God mediate itself through Jesus, in our reverence and adoration of Him, we, too, become like Him. Let us hope the family resemblance will be so certain that the joy of it will surprise us.

Presently our Lord Jesus, at the right hand of God, ministers to us as our Mediator-Priest. He is a high priest after the order of Melchisedec (Hebrews 5:6). In this new service of the Mediator-Teacher, after His ascension, Jesus engages in supplication and succoring. Only after He had conquered death and ascended to the Father's right hand did He enter upon this new sphere of God-ordained support (Hebrews 5:5, 6). The letter to the Hebrews makes it quite clear that Jesus was not a priest when He was upon the earth (Hebrews 7:14). His earthly ministry never involved any activity in the sanctuary. He was a prophet, teacher, mediator, King (though rejected), but never a priest. He did not come from the priestly tribe of Levi. He had no prerogative on earth to administer any Levitical rite or officiate in any service concerning the Temple. When He ascended, however, He assumed the important role God had reserved for Him and delegated to Him (Hebrews 5:5, 6).

His priesthood is a continuing one after the order of Melchisedec and quite unlike the temporal pattern of the Aaronic order. The priesthood ceased with the rending of the veil, when His death and resurrection provided a new and living way into the Holy of Holies (Hebrews 10:20). The ascended Christ now serves in the heavenly temple, and His work for us is intercession. The Intercessor goes between God and us and draws us to God: ". . . he ever liveth to make intercession for them" (Hebrews 7:25). In our pilgrimage, we pupils, guided by a distant but ever close star, raise our sights toward celestial points for navigation. As God's heading-home people we need to know that the Teacher-Guide has his sleepless, watchful eye upon us. He is the Empathizer-Intercessor, who shares our weaknesses and strengthens our frailties. Marvelously, this Intercessor has gone through it all.

The Caring Mediator

How reassuring a word the caring teacher gives—the simple, "I understand." We all crave that. At times we want to talk with someone who has trodden the same tough path; someone who has been in this place and whose heart has been softened by the blows inflicted by the outrageousness of unfairness. I've tried, as a teacher, to listen to sad words students spoke in confidence. "I need someone to understand what's happening to me. Sometimes the pressure seems unbearable, and I'm at the breaking point," and the tears would flow or the anger would fume away. It's an unhappy thing to go through school days and never find a kind, commiserating word. Rebuke and rebuffs from the ones who ought to care become the greatest indignity.

What can we say in support of a teacher whose students' choice word to describe him is *loathe*? He is beyond redemption! One student recalls:

> As long as I live I'll loathe my English teacher. He was the meanest man I knew before I was ten. He was the master of the double insult.
> "Stupid idiot" "silly fool" "dumb blockhead"
> Like a rattlesnake, he always had fresh venom. We were "ignorant illiterates" wasting professional time and public money. His relentless diatribes undercut our self respect and ignited our hate. When he finally fell ill, the whole class celebrated.[17]

It need not be this way.

Theresa was a ninth grader in my own English class. Her grades began to decline, and by mid-year, she was failing. When inspected further, I found she had failing grades in all her courses. What had caused a bright, energetic, and industrious student's performance to nose-dive unexplainably? She had become sullen and inattentive.

I decided to talk with her, and reluctantly she had consented. In my room after school, I told her about my concerns as she gazed absently out the window. "Is there a problem?" I asked. "Is there something wrong that I can help you with? I want to be your friend." Tears began to fall.

"Can I tell you something terrible?" she stammered. "Can I tell you something horrible that's happening to me?"

"I'm willing to listen," I assured her.

"If I tell you, will you still be my friend? Even though you might be disgusted by my story?"

"Friends are for times like these," I answered softly.

In a voice choked with fear and hurt, she poured out an unspeakably vicious account of the sexual and physical abuse she was being subjected to at home. I gasped as she revealed the gruesome details. When she finished, she said in exhaustion, "I don't know what to do. Can you help me? Can *anybody* help me?"

"Friends help friends," I stated confidently. "You bet I'll help you."

For several weeks, I gave her my attention and contacted child-protection agencies and family-support agencies. With little co-operation from school officials, I sought out every advocacy organization I could locate, and I succeeded, after circumventing miles of legal roadblocks, in having her removed from the home and placed in temporary guardianship. It took almost a year to resolve the situation, but eventually, through court intervention, she was assigned to a more wholesome environment.

In all our troubles, we need the heavenly Mediator. God invites us to come into His presence not sheepishly (although sheeplike), but boldly. We come to ". . . the throne of grace, that we may obtain mercy, and find grace to help in time of need" (Hebrews 4:16). The One who commiserates with us experienced the agony of trial. He was *tested* in "all points" as we are, yet we hasten to add, "without sin" (Hebrews 4:15). He is not an indifferent arbiter of disputes but an advocate of the most tender and exquisite compassion.

We often find feelings the most difficult things to deal with. Aching voids within us long to be filled with kind words and gentle caresses; we are sentient beings, not simply cerebral ones. We have feelings and moods and emotions. Schools too often assume students have disembodied minds that need filling or wired circuitry that needs programming. The "affective domain," as educators technically term the emotional area, receives scant consideration.[18] When, in moments of self-reflection, we consider our own personal consciousness, the depth of our identity confronts us. Apart from legions of other people, we are unique— *e pluribus unum*—of many, one! Each of us is idiosyncratically, distinctively, peculiarly singular in his or her existence. Each of us is a once-in-a-lifetime occurrence. Statisticians tell us that it is exponentially improbable that anyone else could be us! No clones exist in God's kingdom. The metaphors of Christ's kingdom are organic, not mechanical. Neither is education a process of insipid conformity, but the development of uniqueness, and in the inner world of the "affect" our uniqueness becomes most poignant. The teacher, in a kind of priestly way, with permission and always courteously, enters the inner sanctum of the sentient self. On the altar, in the soul of souls, that mediator offers sweet incense, and soon the fragrance of a new self-acceptance suffuses and revives the frail being.

Jesus Christ is the "Son of man." That title, which He alone uses of Himself, identifies His power over sin: ". . . The Son of man hath power on earth to forgive sins . . . (Mark 2:10). It also describes His sympathy for sinners. The Gospel of Luke portrays Jesus as the sensitive Man among men. With the physician's attention to human need, Luke notices the Man who mediates for those who live lives of "quiet desperation."

Students who lead such lives fill our schools today. The depression and alarming suicide rate among teenagers testify to the sense of helplessness among them. Martin Seligman's revealing study about depression, development, and death treats the increasing pathological propensity of modern youth.[19] Suicide is now the number-two cause of death among adolescents. As part of the standard in-service schedule schools and teacher programs offer life-threatening-behavior courses. Commissions have been formed to study the causes of suicide, and networks of crisis counselors are available for assistance. My own neighborhood, by most standards a family-oriented, secure community, has experienced the tragedy of four teenage suicides in the last year. We may interpret suicidal acts as cries for help. Tragically and paradoxically, through suicide some seek to affirm the significance of their being. When all support systems seem to crumple and the fragile thread that links meaning to life snaps, often suicide seems the only alternative that attracts attention.

Robert Jay Lifton, a psychiatrist who has devoted much of his professional life to studying people's attitudes and reactions toward death, feels that the act of suicide for many people is the final desperate attempt to affirm their own identities: "Even the despairing suicide of a young person is, in a sense, from his perspective, a search for affirmation. That person tries to say through suicide this is unsatisfactory and by implication there must be some better alternative that I cannot find in my life but that I want to affirm or at least make known by killing myself."[20]

At midnight the telephone's ring jarred me from the nocturnal world of soft pillows and sweet dreams. *Who could possibly be calling at such an unearthly hour?* I thought, disgruntled. I felt tempted to let the phone ring and remain in the comfort of the bed, but dutifully I lumbered across the room, out into the hall, and picked up the receiver. "Hello," I muttered.

"Dr. Kuhlman, you've got to help me. I can't stand it any longer. I'm desperate. I've got a gun—" The shrill, staccato voice pleaded: "You've got to help me. You've got to help me."

"Hold on," I exclaimed, shocked into alertness by the voice's piercing tone. "Who is this? Who's calling?"

The caller gave her name. She was calling from out of state. Although we had had little contact in the last year, I remembered her as a student in one of my classes. She had sat in the back of the room, virtually invisible in the sea of faces. She clung to the walls of the room. The first several weeks of the school term, I scarcely knew she was there, but soon I could identify her by name. She never talked. At times she seemed to live in a remote world of her own. One day later in the semester, she came to my office, wanting to talk. "Come in," I invited her. She asked to make an appointment for another time, as though she had second thoughts about coming. We scheduled an appointment for the following week, and she returned and sat nervously fidgeting with her purse. Something I had said in class prompted her to seek me out. I had attempted to relate identity to the acceptance we have in Christ. She remembered that I stated that in Christ,

God grants us unconditional acceptance. Sonship is something we start from, I had said, not something we strive for.

That meeting was the first of many sessions, over several years, when we talked together and I tried to counsel her. She related intimate details of her not-so-happy homelife and her few relationships. Plagued with a weak self-image and low self-esteem, she saw herself as worthless. She'd had few successes in life. During the next two years, almost weekly she came down to talk and seemed to gain some assurance of God's love for her. However, she had great difficulty in getting love for herself. There was nothing lovely about her, she insisted. In time, we broke through that barrier, and she made some modest gains in self-acceptance and confidence. September came, but she didn't return to college, and I lost contact with her. Time went by without a word—and then that phone call.

I hung up at 2:00 A.M. Her near-hysterical behavior subsided, and soon she talked coherently and rationally. I reassured her of my concern and God's love. I listened as she talked, nonstop, about her worthlessness. If only she had something to live for. I tried to convince her that life was not futile. "Don't make any decisions during the night," I pleaded. "I realize life looks like a blind alley to you now, but wait until morning. If you'd like, I'll ride out to see you. I have friends out that way. I'll put them in touch with you."

Mostly, she wanted to talk. I had been trained enough in counseling techniques to know that listening was the best thing to do. *Be affirming. Be reassuring. Give her a sense of hope, but above all, let her talk*, I repeated to myself.

After she had talked herself out, she settled down and maintained she would be all right. I gave her the name of a counselor friend of mine in the area. She promised to call me back the next day. When she did, she said things looked better. That was the last thing I heard from her.

The world can become a lonely and frightening place for many students, and they fear direct contact with it. It is hostile, cold and uncaring, they say. Teachers need to mediate between the threatening world and the frightened students. But teachers can never mediate unless they become sensitive to students and can gain their trust and confidence.

The Lord Jesus Christ, the accessible Man, has demonstrated that He can be trusted and that He will not violate confidences. Luke (unlike Matthew) traces the genealogy of the Lord back to the first man, Adam (Luke 3:38). Luke tells us about Jesus' early development, His time in the Temple, and his concern for infirmities, sickness, and sorrow. Scholars have suggested that Luke wrote his Gospel especially for the gentile world and for Greeks in particular. They had always sought the perfect man—the perfect gentleman. In song and legend they had idolized the virtues of the paragon—a man, mortal but godlike, embodying all the virtues of virility and manly sensitivity, who could mediate between them and life's tragedy—someone like Homer's Achilles, a champion, but without his vulnerability and vices. And One appears who is not simply godlike, but very God, Himself—the Mediator between God and men—the Man, Christ Jesus.

As the Mediator-Teacher, Jesus is also the "medicator." He never leaves our needs unattended, for pain results from unmet needs. Created in the image of God, man cannot tolerate indefinite, protracted periods of privation, especially in those needs that are akin to his Godlikeness. Lack of physiological-survival needs produces pain, but the lack of provision for the soul's and spirit's needs produces pain beyond endurance. William Glasser, noted psychiatrist-educator, has analyzed the responses to prolonged, unabated pain and concluded that eventually preoccupation with the pain itself precludes all other considerations. Forgetting need itself, the hurting person directs all energies and actions toward finding relief. Addictions, despair, mental instability, and other reactions may all emerge as anodynes for the pain.[21]

One of the critical functions of teachers as mediators is to attend to students' needs. Needs unfulfilled interfere with vital learning. Our Lord continues, in His intercessory-advocacy role, to make provisions for us "in time of need." In His departure from the Mount of Olives, when the Lord ascended to heaven, the Mediator ". . . lifted up his hands and blessed them. And it came to pass, while he blessed them, he was parted from them, and carried up into heaven'' (Luke 24:50, 51). The joyful disciple-students knew that the Man who came to be Mediator had accomplished His purposes upon earth. Now this very Man would appear in the presence of God *for them* (Hebrews 9:24). His mighty and merciful work of advocacy and intercession would provide them with the strength and sensitivity they would need to carry on their ministries. For us today, the same assurance pertains, through our Mediator, who taught us and continues to intercede for us.

8
COMING TO A NEEDY WORLD

For even the Son of man came not to be ministered unto,
but to minister, and to give his life a ransom for many

Mark 10:45

A Poem to a Teacher
I cannot write poetry, yet how else
can I tell.
How tell of this man among men—
not tall, not fair;
Bringing no gifts, speaking no harsh
words.
How tell of the miracle he wrought:
the loosening of the cords binding
my soul, the cutting of the
strings which draw tight the
shutters of my mind.
How else can I tell you of this
listening heart.[1]

"**B**ut he that is greatest among you shall be your servant" (Matthew 23:11). The hypocritical behavior of the scribes and Pharisees (which belied their public proclamations) prompted this remark from the Lord. As teachers of the Law, the scribes proudly traced their ancestry through Ezra back to Moses; they sat in "Moses' seat" (Matthew 23:2). Upon themselves they took the sacred task of keeping the Law of Moses before the people, and sadly, this noble entitlement degenerated into a futile exercise of straining gnats and swallowing camels (Matthew 23:24). For these "blind guides," this exalted function as guardians and disseminators of God's holy decrees had become nothing more than tedium, as the scribes spun their entangling web of interpretation and commentary. In time, the status of the scribes was elevated and soon, along with the ritualistic Pharisees, they became an effete, privileged caste, serving no useful purpose. Their position of godly leadership had degenerated into self-serving indulgence.

Though the scribes loved to be on display and they enjoyed the benefits that came with their office, they contributed nothing useful to the people whom they purported to teach. The "upper crust" of the professoriat, tenured for life, with no accountability, these parasites lived off the people, providing no services of substance and parading about, living lavishly. Having achieved celebrity status, they maintained it by keeping the people slavish to their interpretation and ignorant of the liberating truth: "For they bind heavy burdens and grievous to be borne, and lay them on men's shoulders; but they themselves will not move them with one of their fingers" (Matthew 23:4). The Lord Jesus had nothing but the harshest rebuke for them.

The Ministering Teacher

The teacher from God is a *minister*—one who comes to a world where *need* is the dominant theme. He traffics in the midst of humanity, where misery and pain prevail. Recognizing the priority of ministry, the true teacher answers the call into a "helping profession" in which he provides a storehouse of support upon which students can draw.

Jesus: Teacher-Servant

Our Lord led a life of ministry. Often we refer to teaching as *a* ministry, but more correctly, teaching *is* ministry; service and a sense of mission are integral aspects of it. At the outset of His ministry, the Lord Jesus received and joyfully accepted the mandate to service. In His hometown of Nazareth, He arose in the synagogue meeting and read the prophecy about Himself from Isaiah: ". . . And when he had opened the book, he found the place where it was written, The spirit of the Lord is upon me, because he hath anointed me to preach the gospel to the poor; he hath sent me to heal the broken hearted, to preach deliverance to the captives, and recovering of sight to the blind, to set at liberty them that are bruised, To preach the acceptable year of the Lord" (Luke 4:17–19).

Later, in the midst of an active and energy-draining profusion of service to others, Matthew records that unlike the scribes and Pharisees Jesus sought anonymity. He cites Isaiah as the witness to this commitment to unheralded ministry: "Behold my servant, whom I have chosen; my beloved, in whom my soul is well pleased: I will put my spirit upon him, and he shall shew judgment to the Gentiles. He shall not strive, nor cry; neither shall any man hear his voice in the streets. A bruised reed shall he not break, and smoking flax shall he not quench, till he send forth judgment unto victory" (Matthew 12:18–20).

In sharp contrast to the teachers of the Law, the Teacher-Servant neither sought nor desired fame or public acclaim. Jesus "went about doing good" (Acts 10:38), yet never showed a hint of selfishness or self-seeking glory in any of His activities. When he ". . . took upon him the form of a servant . . ." (Philippians 2:7), He volitionally set aside any claim to self-assertion. He became submissive (although never subordinate) to the Father, and that was His key to success. No one can understand the public ministry of the Lord apart from the realization that He never sought personal promotion.

How unlike practice today! In an age when we so viciously covet the pinnacle, the pathway to the top is strewn with wreckage—fatalities of this rapacious quest. Even in academia, we face the problem. Titles and tenure! Status and scholarly recognition! Certainly such things are not entirely improper in themselves; indeed we *need* to make distinctions. Society has various needs, and we differentiate people by the needs they fill. In fact, such distinctions actually encourage fraternity, as Richard Weaver has noted, because only people who are aware of their differences can align in some mutually beneficial arrangement. "It is a matter of common observation, too, that people meet most easily when they know their position. If their work and authority are defined they can proceed on fixed assumptions and conduct themselves without embarrassment toward inferior and superior."[2]

Fraternity, uniting distinct parts, forms the basis of any organic social order. That does not mean we call the distinctions into question; instead we question the basis on which we make distinctions and the social use to which we put them. We must not set ourselves a goal of conquest, but one of service. Our Lord reminds us (and we need regular reminders) that teaching is a gift we must use for the good of others. Benefit does not come from denying the gift, for that would rob the Body of Christ of many benefits. Nor should Christians deny gifted teachers their proper recognition and respect (Romans 13:7). Clearly distinctions should not be blurred. Jesus told His disciples: "Ye call me Master and Lord: and ye say well; for so I am" (John 13:13). The Lord did not engage in false humility when He stooped to take the servant's place. Servanthood rests upon strength.

Only the teacher who possesses a sure sense of identity and

commitment can serve others. Back in the days of my high-school teaching, one male student made an unflattering comment about a girl in the class. I let him know that I would not tolerate scurrilous remarks. He looked at me, grinned devilishly, and said: "But that's what she is, Mr. Ed." (This happened during the era of the T.V. program about a talking horse with that name!) In a split second, I calculated all my options. How should I react? My reputation was on the line. I had to save face. Dare I let him get away with that remark before the whole class? Without hesitation, I snatched a chalk-dust-laden eraser from the blackboard and flung it, with pinpoint accuracy, inches above his head. The eraser hit the wall behind him, and a cloud of dust wreathed his head like fallout from an explosion and settled like dandruff in his hair. I expected affirming laughter for my chivalrous act, but the class greeted the episode with disturbed annoyance. What I saw as a demonstration of decisiveness they interpreted as personal insecurity. I had sunk to the level of the class culprit. Personal inadequacy prompted retaliation, and the class recognized the flaw. I should have been above that sort of thing, and that experience helped me reexamine my own identity and resolve some of the ambiguity in my life. With this new knowledge came an opportunity for personal and professional assessment and a chance to grow.

As the Ministering-Teacher, our Lord Jesus was not a spineless, obsequious, indecisive lackey, who pandered to the whims of the fickle crowd. He never cowered or cringed in anyone's presence. Told that Herod sought to kill Him, Christ replied: "Go ye, and tell that fox . . ." (Luke 13:32). Standing before Pilate, who represented the power of Imperial Rome, Jesus declared without a hint of fear: "Thou couldest have no power at all against me, except it were given thee from above . . ." (John 19:11). This Servant in submission to the Father carries Himself with strength and serenity, and His accusers wilt before Him.

The servant qualities of Christ are filtered through the lens of Mark's Gospel. Like a prism refracting the rays from the sun, this slim Gospel focuses the common color of Jesus' ministry as Servant. In crisp, uncluttered style, paying no heed to ancestry, the Gospel quickly brings the Servant-Teacher onstage, and in rapid succession, using the instructive term "immediately,"[3] narrates and enumerates the series of servant tasks He undertakes. Mark uses a more forceful and less leisurely term (in contrast with Matthew and Luke) to show the Servant's eagerness: "the spirit driveth him into the wilderness" (Mark 1:12). Christ does not reluctantly confront Satan; on the contrary, He is eager for the encounter and so is "thrust out" (Greek: *ekballo*).

Mark provides us with the movements of the Ministering-Teacher, who goes from place to place and from need to need; his Gospel presents the Teacher who *touches* rather than the Teacher who *talks*. Words are few. The Servant avoids verbosity and teaches by attending to needs, coupling kindness and compassion with ability. The other synoptic Gospels record more extensive verbiage in comparable settings than Mark does. A comparison of the Gospels, using a red-letter edition of the Bible, highlights this contrast.

Understandably, Mark, who wrote the book under the guidance of Simon Peter, could recognize and record the "ministry motif" of the Lord Jesus. Mark, after all, had accompanied Paul and Barnabas on their first missionary journey: "And when they were at Salamis, they preached the word of God . . . and they had also John [Mark] to their minister" (Acts 13:5). He had failed, however, in the initial ministry and defected when the assignment became perilous. In preparing for his second journey, Paul feuded with Barnabas over the role Mark should play in the venture. Heated controversy resulted in separation, and Mark accompanied his uncle, Barnabas ("son of encouragement"), and began a serious apprenticeship as a minister. Mark learned his lessons well under the tutelage of Barnabas. When the aged apostle Paul was imprisoned in Rome, he called for Mark: ". . . Take Mark, and bring him with thee: for he is profitable to me for the ministry" (2 Timothy 4:11). The time with Barnabas and Peter ("Marcus my son" [1 Peter 5:13]) was time well spent.

Mark depicts Christ as the Teacher-Minister. With an eye alert to the servant attitude, he pays particular attention to the ministering character of Christ. In parsimonious style the Gospel writer peels away layers and gives us the terse, unwordy revelation of Isaiah's prophesied Servant, who "hath borne our griefs, and carried our sorrows . . ." (Isaiah 53:4). Mark never lingers at a scene. This is not the servant's prerogative. The prophet Elisha commanded his servant, Gehazi: ". . . Go thy way: if thou meet any man, salute him not; and if any salute thee, answer him not again . . ." (2 Kings 4:29). Go where you are directed. Do what you are commanded and return. Neither loiter nor lounge.

Power for Service

The minister-teacher must be commissioned and empowered. At our Lord's baptism, the Spirit of God came upon Him and He was able (as He had been eager) to carry out the Father's commission. The Spirit's envelopment brought enduement. Impotence accompanies presumption. Jesus never failed in any of His ministering efforts. At times, the disciples could not meet needs, but never their Lord. The consensus concerning His ministry was: ". . . He hath done all things well . . ." (Mark 7:37). In the upper room for ten days the disciples waited patiently for the Spirit's enduement, because they knew they could not effectively minister without His power. On Pentecost, flames of fire lit their tongues, and ignited a conflagration that consumed the world.

Early in His ministry, Jesus met the need of Peter's mother-in-law, who lay ill with a fever. The Lord responded lovingly. Mark reports that "he came and took her by the hand, and lifted her up . . ." (Mark 1:31). Geoffrey Bull interprets this as a reference to Christ's *ability*.[4] Ability begets ability, because after her healing, she "ministered unto them" (Mark 1:31). The Ministering-Teacher makes ministers of us.

Places of Service

The English word *deacon* is derived from the commonly used Greek word that has been transliterated into our language: *diakonos*. Robert Anderson does not accept the term *deacon* as a title.[5] Typically modern churches use the term to indicate an office, and members of the church with appropriate qualifications are elected or appointed to the office. The more liturgical churches incorporate this office into their hierarchy (diaconate). However, the word more correctly refers to a function, and ministers of the first century served in the Word and in good works. In Acts, chapter 6, when the church faced a problem with the needs of the neglected widows, they singled out seven men to serve those needs, to minister to that particular work. Peter and the other apostles felt their ministry should be more effectively devoted to the Word (Acts 6:1–5). Ministering covered a variety of functions and activities that fulfilled needs. To Timothy, Paul outlined the comprehensive nature of such duties: "If thou put the brethren in remembrance of these things, thou shalt be a good minister of Jesus Christ . . ." (1 Timothy 4:6).

Stephen stands out as a deacon who did more than the custodial chores normally assigned to that office today. "Full of faith and power," he "did great wonders and miracles among the people" and clearly had a teacher's grasp of God's Word. He could recite lengthy portions of the Old Testament (Acts 6:8; 7:2–53). His ministry extended beyond the business of routine church matters and encompassed teaching that identified him as a man of exceptional skill and knowledge.

The deacon's service may come in unlikely places and in unlikely forms. When Corrie ten Boom was imprisoned in Scheveningen, she was unable to read because her glasses had been damaged. But that simple service was performed by "a kind teacher with me who daily reads to me . . . and I enjoy it. She also combed my hair . . . and she is now writing for me."[6]

Service is multifaceted in its design. Sometimes the hurried stride of the teacher hastens him to the all too frequent calamities that occur in the classroom. At other times, its disciplined reluctance keeps a distance and, against natural impulse, waits and waits and waits.

> *God doth not need*
> *Either man's work or His own gifts. Who best*
> *Bear His mild yoke, they serve Him best: His state*

is kingly; thousands at His bidding speed
And post o'er land and ocean without rest;
They also serve who only stand and wait.[7]

Visions of Service

The servant-teacher (unlike the hireling) realizes that education has never been a financially profitable profession and refuses to calculate its benefits solely in terms of profit and loss. The ledger book mind-set does not fit well in the classroom. The meager salary I received in my early teaching days was not my incentive for becoming a teacher. And the Sunday-school teachers who serve sacrificially do not minister with the prospect of material reward. Sometimes others do not reciprocate the kindness of a motivated teacher, but satisfaction comes from serving. Servant-teachers concur with the apostle Paul and announce that "the love of Christ constrains us" (*see* 2 Corinthians 5:14). How can we explain ministers like Mother Teresa of Calcutta unless we realize they serve simply and solely for love of Jesus.

> Tell them . . . we are here for Jesus. We serve Jesus in the poor. We nurse Him, feed Him, clothe Him, visit Him, comfort Him in the poor, the abandoned, the sick, the orphans, the dying. But all we do, our prayer, our work, our suffering is for Jesus. Our life has no other reason or motivation. This is the point many people do not understand. I serve Jesus twenty-four hours a day, whatever I do is for Him. . . . Without Jesus our life would be meaningless, incomprehensible; Jesus explains our life. . . . tell them, WE DO IT FOR JESUS.[8]

Mother Teresa has gained an international reputation for sacrifical service to others, and she exemplifies the values and virtues of the minister-teacher. Her life has been an act of devotion, and she has attracted pupils who share her commitment and compassion. However, she holds her classes in the cluttered corners of life; she sets up her school among the sick. The healing ministry of this teacher-servant has touched Calcutta.

Ministry is medicinal. Teaching and touching are inseparable. The word *good* fits the Samaritan because he took time to stop and attend the mangled lives along the fringes of life's busy thoroughfares. Neither the priest nor Levite stopped to help the hurting. Fear of defilement kept them at a distance, and they viewed the sorry sights from the "other side" of the road. The true minister unfearingly trespasses the invisible line that separates the social strata. Teachers with balm and ointment for wounds and putrefying sores cross over, unafraid (Luke 10:29–37). Goodness gives of itself. The Lord Jesus, the great Giver, is regularly and rightfully called *good*.

But good, it seems, has fallen out of fashion. Though many claim greatness, few make goodness their goal. A teacher must be a *good* person. Seldom is this quality specifically identified among the criteria suggested for teachers. Skill, competency, credentials—all these have places on the standard lists. We evaluate teacher effectiveness by these guidelines, but *goodness* is conspicuously absent. Goodness extends itself beyond traditional boundaries; convention cannot circumscribe it. Jesus always reaches out beyond the walls that barricade people within their private prisons. When blind Bartimaeus calls, Jesus stands still (Mark 10:49). When a woman with an incurable illness crawls to touch his garment, He halts (Luke 8:43–48). Lepers, gentiles, and women (the pariah classes) experienced His goodness.

In Jesus' day, people never visited Gadara, one region around the Sea of Galilee. It had no tourist attractions. You might call it the "other side"—the other side of the tracks, the wrong side of town, the place respectable people never went. Teachers never took field trips *there*! Someone *might* point to it across the sea (about seven or eight miles away), but no self-respecting person would venture there. But the Minister-Teacher instructed His disciples to board the boat and directed their course to that *very* spot—to the other side. A rusty mooring—a decrepit dock in need of repair—weeds and vermin.[9] This Teacher was the first in many years to make His way from the safe shores of Capernaum to that desolate, God-forsaken outback. Graveyards for the dead and pigsties for swine and strange noises unnerved the neighbors. Rumor had it that a madman ran loose among the ruins. Without trepidation, the Servant of God came with His ministry of love and message of liberation, and soon He freed part of the promised land from pigs and demons.[10] The wild man of the tombs now sat sanely and saintly at the feet of Jesus (Luke 8:26–35). At twilight, the Lord returned across the lake to continue His ministry and left a native son who had learned the lesson of liberty and would now minister in his own neighborhood.

Paul tells Timothy, "The servant of the Lord must not strive; but be gentle unto all men, apt to teach, patient, In meekness instructing those that oppose . . ." (2 Timothy 2:24–25). Gentleness, patience, and meekness are indispensable qualities of the ministering teacher. In Ephesians 4:11, Paul identifies one of the chief gifts to the church—the pastor-teacher. A sensitive pastor is a teacher; a true teacher is a pastor. The terms are related and the tasks are inseparable. A "pastor" (Greek: *poimen*) shepherds his flock. The teacher-servant is the teacher-shepherd. No simile more aptly illustrates and exemplifies the ministry of the teacher. In the world of Palestine, everyone knew what shepherds were and what they did. *Shepherd* communicates the fundamental qualities of caring, compassion, and guidance; shepherds *superintend* the ways and welfare of the sheep. Using this imagery, Peter, familiar with pastoral scenes throughout Galilee, refers to church elders: "The elders which are among you I exhort, who am also an elder . . . Feed the flock of God which is among you, taking the oversight . . . willingly . . ." (1 Peter 5:1, 2). In similar fashion, Paul called ". . . the elders of the church" from Ephesus and exhorted them to "Take heed therefore unto yourselves, and to all the flock, over . . . which the Holy Ghost hath made you overseers, to feed the church of God . . ." (Acts 20:17, 28). The terms *elder* and *overseer* suggest similar shepherd care and nurturance. The elders were to be teachers as well: ". . . apt to teach" (1 Timothy 3:2). These terms suggest the full range of ministry.

The Shepherd-Ministry

In Dundee, Scotland, early in the last century, a young pastor gained a reputation for his sensitive, shepherd ministry. Possessing scholarly capabilities (he studied Greek and Hebrew at Edinburgh University), he combined academic keenness in teaching with a shepherd's sensitivity that made him unique among his fellow clergy. St. Peter's in Dundee, the church of his highly successful ministry, gained a wide reputation during his tenure. Robert Murray McCheyne suffered from frequent illness and did not survive his thirtieth birthday, but in his short career, he unshakably established himself among the memorable shepherd-pastors. In correspondence to his congregation, he delighted in using fond phrases of intimacy for "his flock." Typical of these affectionate epistles is this pastoral letter: "To all of you, my dear flock. . . . Even in the wildest storms the sky is not all dark. . . . Yet some of you have felt that His own hand was leading us like a flock. . . . I am permitted to go in secret to God, my exceeding joy; and while meditating His praise, I can make mention of you all in my prayers and give thanks for the little flock. . . ."[11]

Prior to his extended mission to the Holy Land, McCheyne wrote to his congregation using the sweet similes that expressed his shepherd-heart of love: "To all you my dear flock. . . . Oh, you that can pray that I come back a holy minister—a shepherd not to lead the flock by voice only, but to *walk* before them in the way of life. . . . Dear children of God I now cast you on Him who cast you on me when I was ordained over you. He said to me 'feed my sheep . . . feed my lambs . . . feed my sheep.' "[12]

Lambs need to be fed and led. Learners need to be taught. McCheyne, quick of mind and quiet of heart, brought together the virtues of the shepherd-teacher. Therefore, a teacher performs service as shepherd stewardship. He leads students in and out, guiding and guarding them; they are fed and returned to the protection of the fold. The shepherd-teacher knows students' idiosyncrasies and with diligence attends to their learning and maturity.

The Lord Jesus, the Good Shepherd, precedes His sheep when

they leave the sheepfold (John 10:4). The Teacher-Shepherd always leads. As the Lord journeyed from Galilee to Jerusalem (with the cross His ultimate destiny), the disciples displayed amazement that Jesus took the initiative: "And they were in the way going up to Jerusalem; and Jesus went before them: and they were amazed . . ." (Mark 10:32). Jesus never lingered behind; He was always in the vanguard.

Called by Name

The Good Shepherd "leads his dear children along." The sheep are prone to wander off unadvisedly, but He goes and reclaims them. Though He may have one hundred of them, each is important (Luke 15:4). He calls them by name. Nothing is more personal to us—so identifiably ours—as our names. Dr. Leo Buscaglia, noted educator, has told the tearful story of a vivacious, attractive student who took her own life. Usually punctual and present in Buscaglia's class of 500 students, she was absent two consecutive weeks. Buscaglia asked the students who sat near her if they had any information about her. To his astonishment and dismay, no one even knew her name. He later discovered the tragic truth of that twenty-two-year-old student's suicide.

When a substitute teacher asked a boy in the class for his name, he replied, "Mahatma Gandhi." The class laughed uproariously. The teacher reassured that student that Mahatma Gandhi was a good person to be named after, and the class became calm.[13] That teacher knew that names, remembered or forgotten, admired or scorned, can cause pleasure or pain. That's why dehumanizing places (prisons and prison camps) substitute numbers for names. The final insult—the great indignity—is to be stripped of uniqueness. Losing one's name means losing one's identity—becoming invisible. In a world of anonymity, where identification and code numbers proliferate, names are in serious jeopardy. Victor Frankl recalls the chilling numbness of namelessness in a Nazi concentration camp.

It did not matter which, since each of them was nothing but a number. On their admission to the camp (at least this was the method in Auschwitz) all their documents had been taken from them, together with their other possessions. . . . The authorities were interested only in their captives' numbers. These numbers were often tattoed on their skin, and also had to be sewn to a certain spot on the trousers, jacket or coat. Any guard who wanted to make a charge against a prisoner just glanced at his number . . .; he never asked for his name.[14]

Society and sometimes schools cipher people. Names are erased and replaced with a less cumbersome, more easily pronounceable substitute, including the degrading, "Hey you!" As a teacher and counselor in schools, I tried to learn every student's name and let him hear it at least once a day. As a college teacher, I still do. I thought about all the nonentities in schools and wrote this poem for an educational journal:

Are you
Client? Counselee? Patient?
Terms that conveniently cage you
in precise pathological positions
and permit you to be treated.
I prescribe perfunctorily and say,
with clinical detachment,
"You are healed."

Are you
Self? Significant Other? Actor?
Depersonalized designations that
stylize, systematize, and structuralize
into juxtaposition as I search for
a function for you. Until then,
I pronounce you nameless.

Are you
Variable? Datum? Cipher?
Neatly keypunched on a data deck.
Measurable. Manageable. Manipulable.
Command the computer and you are
processed, percentiled, and profiled.
You are graphed, analyzed, and numbered
among the norms. But I refrain from
folding, stapling, or touching.
Computer courtesy.

Are you . . . who are you?
Tiring taxonomies and typologies
with procrustean simplicity shrink wrap you
with hermetic efficiency and
render you sterile. Upon you
neither germs nor genius grows.

You are you.
And so I disregard files and folders
and print outs. I ask your name.
You disclose.
I tell my name. I disclose.
We know and are known.[15]

I suppose we all recall with fondness those teachers who took time to learn our names and pronounce them properly. They said them in just the right way, to let us know that each of us was unique and special. We respond to the right kind of name calling.

The Lord Jesus, the Shepherd-Teacher, calls His own by name. No one is anonymous or simply numbered in His school. He calls us always with the inflection of affection. Our names are ever on His lips, and He speaks them with significance. He never mispronounces. He makes no mistakes among us. Our names are written in the Lamb's book of Life (Revelation 21:27).

King David, the sovereign-shepherd, knew life in meadow and manor. He never forgot his early years among the flocks. God brought him from the obscurity of grazing grounds to the royal throne, and he traded his shepherd's staff for a king's scepter. "He chose David also his servant, and took him from the sheepfolds: From following the ewes great with young he brought him to feed Jacob his people, and Israel his inheritance. So he fed them according to the integrity of his heart; and guided them by the skilfulness of his hands" (Psalms 78:70–72).

David's "greater Son," the Shepherd-King, leads and feeds us in "green pastures" and "beside still waters." Whether food for the stomach or soul, we eat the finest wheat and drink the sweetest wine.

The Careful Shepherd

Good teachers do not become careless about what their students consume. Careful planning and preparation provide an appetizing and nourishing array of courses in the curriculum. Teachers dare not pander to the baser tastes of students and feed them only what their sweet teeth crave. Sensation—titillation—please the eye and palate, but leave the heart hollow. With cultivated artistry and the connoisseur's eye for what is profitable, the teacher spreads the "table before them." Dull, monotonous menus of irrelevancies do little to whet the appetite for further learning. Integrity of heart and skillfulness of hand, combined, enhance learning, and good teachers have them both.

In his book subtitled *A Spirituality of Education*, Parker Palmer identifies three sources of education: control, curiosity, and compassion. Education for control leads to exploitation. If generated by curiosity, education becomes capricious and ends up as manipulation. If compassion motivates, however, it will result in edification. Palmer writes:

> The goal of a knowledge arising from love is the reunification and reconstruction of broken selves and worlds. A knowledge born of compassion aims not at exploitation and manipulating creation but at reconciling the world to itself. The mind motivated by com-

passion reaches out to know as the heart reaches out to love.

. . . Curiosity and control create a knowledge that distances us from each other and the world, allowing us to use what we know as a plaything and to play the game by our own self-serving rules. But a knowledge that springs from love will implicate us in a web of life; it will wrap the knower and the known in compassion, in a bond of awesome responsibility as well as transforming joy; it will call us to involvement, mutuality and accountability.[16]

The servant-teacher motivated by compassion will be, supremely, of a quiet spirit and gentle demeanor. With muted tones, Mark's Gospel paints the portrait of the Minister-Teacher: quietly and quickly, He attends to His teaching; without arrogance (but not without ability), He moves decisively, content to let the commendations be few.

Gently and kindly our blessed Lord taught them that the true greatness consists of humility and lowly service. . . . What God values is humble service. So many want to do "great" things. The way to do great things is to begin doing little things. . . . May we seek to imitate Him.[17]

The apostle Paul enjoins teacher-ministers to wait upon their ministry (Romans 12:7). They "wait" in the sense of serving, even as a waiter "waits upon tables." Teachers must be first and foremost servants, and goodness must precede greatness: ". . . Whosoever will be great among you, shall be your minister" (Mark 10:43). The teacher's touch of merciful ministry complements the talk of mastery. In Christ, the Minister-Teacher, these qualities and commitments come together perfectly and profitably.

9
LEADING THE WAY

For I have given you an example, that ye should do as I have done to you.

John 13:15

Example is notoriously more potent than precept.[1]

I wanted to offer a supreme model to the man who struggles. . . . Christ suffered pain, and since then pain has been sanctified. . . . Every obstacle in his journey became a milestone, an occasion for further triumph. We have a model in front of us now, a model who blazes our trail and gives us strength.[2]

Our history teacher had an indelible impact on my life. Though old, he was contemporary and passionate. He loved life and art. He enjoyed translating the lessons of the past into guidelines for the future. He picked the bones of history delicately, treating its heroes with reverence. A refined and eloquent speaker, he was the epitome of the gentleman-scholar.[3]

My favorite teacher, Mr. Daniel, was a most unforgettable character. He took time to know us. He encouraged us to talk about our lives, about our homes and family, our wishes, our fears, our frustrations. In a short time, he knew me better than did my parents. . . . He listened to us, and we had something to say. He rarely raised his voice or used harsh words. He never attacked. He pointed out what needed to be done and stood by ready to give help.[4]

Example is worth more than words, the old adage says. Seeing something lived out before us confirms what others say. The English word *teacher* comes from the Anglo-Saxon word that means "to show." The teacher is the "show-er." In order to attain the goals of instruction, students must have before them an exemplar of the lesson. They must see a flesh-and-blood manifestation. One student's evaluation of her model-teacher highlights how he became an on-stage example for his students: "Our drama teacher was a true poet. . . . He captivated our imagination and captured our hearts. He never criticized, he coaxed. He never pushed, he persuaded. He never insulted, he inspired. With sensitivity, he taught us to contrast drama and life, to emulate performance and character. Through his efforts, I came to appreciate and to choose the theatre as my life."[5]

As Shakespeare said: "All the world's a stage," and educational shows go on not only in classrooms. Homes are theaters as well, and parents provide rich role models. Their influences early in their children's lives form the character and start the bent of the twig. Mozart's music began under his father's tutelage, and he learned to play the harpsichord so well that he toured Europe as a child prodigy, giving concerts. By the age of seven, Mozart had learned to compose sonatas. Beethoven's father showed him how to play the violin and clavier at the age of four.

Children observe and emulate. Life is played out before them on the small stages of family and friends, and the show they see determines who and what they will be. Sometimes the scenes turn into tragedies.

The Bible documents sordid stories where children "played out" the scenes of their childhood. Lot's daughters followed the ways of their father and mother (Genesis 19:16–38). Absalom alienated his father, David, who stood by, helpless to act because of his own infidelity (2 Samuel 15:10–12). Family lines are hardened by the examples of ancestors.

But the glad account of sanguine outcomes is equally evident. Timothy could trace his faith and love for the Scriptures back to his mother and grandmother (2 Timothy 1:5). The sons of Zebedee had their spiritual sensitivity first developed by their father's godly example.

The record of a father's pious influence upon his son is chronicled in the intimate account of Edmund Gosse. Raised and educated by his widowed father, in Victorian England, Gosse describes the impact his father made upon him and upon his subsequent life and career. Gosse acquired scholarly interests from his father, who had developed a well-earned reputation as a scientist and illustrator. Although Edmund rejected much of the narrow orthodoxy of his father, he continued to be influenced throughout his life by the piety that permeated all life in the Gosse home. Edmund's literary interests and successes were to a great extent formed and fashioned by his parents and their nurturance. He became a noted writer, lecturer, and professor and the acquaintance of many London notables of his time. Among many honors he received, he was knighted in 1925.[6]

The Model-Teacher

The Lord Jesus comes before us as the Model-Teacher, whom we must emulate. He comes in the fullness of His humanity so that we can see the lesson lived out before our very eyes. "The Word was made flesh, and dwelt among us . . . ," John declares (John 1:14). In the pages of Scripture, a reality we can behold and hold repeatedly confronts us. Christ's life was a theater in which we see redemptive drama unfolding as we view attentively (one of our words for viewing comes from the Greek word, *theaomi*—"theater"). The Incarnation provides us with deity clothed in human flesh. The apostle Paul identifies this as a *great* mystery: "And without controversy great is the mystery of godliness: God was manifest in the flesh . . ." (1 Timothy 3:16). Christ came not in angel guise. He entered into human time, through Abraham's seed (Hebrews 2:16). He who had been in the ". . . form of God . . . was made in the likeness of men: And being found in fashion as a man, he humbled himself . . ." (Philippians 2:6–8). Implicit in this great and gracious act of condescension was the full manifestation of the "Godhead bodily" (Colossians 2:9). ". . . We beheld his glory . . . ," John gasps in amazement (John 1:14).

What is God like: What attributes does God possess? What is the essence of the nature of the inexhaustible Being of God? These queries surface perennially as sages and skeptics alike ponder the ineffable presence of deity. If God appeared among us, what could we expect to see? How would He act? Would He live so differently from the teaching He gave? Could we expect from Him a correspondence between rhetoric and reality—a congruence between word and deed? Would there be an affinity, for *this* Teacher, between the agenda He prescribed for His followers and the one by which He lived? Far too many self-styled teachers do not follow their own dictums.

Show and Tell

The Teacher from eternity comes not just to tell, but to show. He provides the paramount object lesson. If He talks of things divine and heavenly, He talks with integrity, for He has come from heaven's realm. If He talks of things earthly, He speaks with similar credibility because He trafficked in the avenues of human weal and woe. The roads He walked were dust laden, and His feet calloused. The Judean sun bronzed His face as it did His neighbor's. He went in and out, up and down, and was, Himself, the great Object Lesson. The Teacher and teaching are one. As Marshall McLuhan has so wittily phrased it: "The medium is the message."[7]

"No man hath seen God at any time . . . ," we are informed by the disciple who rested on Jesus' bosom (John 1:18). But this One—the Son—has come to "declare him." Our Lord comes not from the head of God, to our mind's idle curiosity, although what He proposes is unquestionably the most reasonable of programs. In ancient mythology, the goddess Athena sprang, full-formed, from the head of Zeus, and her symbol was the unclean owl—a bird of worldly wisdom. In startling contrast to mere myth, Jesus, symbolized only by clean animals (dove, lamb), was sent from the very heart of the Father, to declare God. The term John uses, translated "declare," is the Greek word, *exegeomai*, which means "to lead out" or "rehearse." Christ is the great *exegesis* of the Father! As a scholar takes a passage of literature, unravels its intention, so God's Son, in Himself, is the declaration of God, the great Guide to the Father.

The labyrinth of King Minos, in ancient Crete, was a maze of passageways and tunnels. Once entrapped within, no wanderer could find his way out of the complex of bends and dead ends. When Theseus became trapped there and awaited his doom, Ariadne, the daughter of Minos, quite literally threaded her way through the maze and thereby brought Theseus to safety. From this ancient myth comes our word *clue*. Ariadne found her way out by following the clue. Reverently we say that Christ is the Clue to God. He is the One who wends our way through the maze of man's own making and guides us to God. By becoming the Model-Teacher, He demonstrates both the path to God and the very Person of God.

A good teacher communicates his mind to his students by the example of his life. The mind that was in Christ Jesus modeled a life of humility, service, and suffering. Setting aside the prerogatives of deity, He "made himself of no reputation" (Philippians 2:7). His deity was veiled but *never* voided!

Current studies in the psychology of learning, using the "social modeling theory," support the notion that we learn behavior by copying a significant model.[8] Learners begin to copy actions of teachers and respond to situations as the teachers do. Our Lord used that strategy as He showed His disciple-students how God would act—yea, how God *was* acting! Their imitation of Him was not simply the sincerest form of flattery; it was the basis for their own development. By emulation, the disciples acquired behaviors that betrayed their commitment to their Master and Model. From the priests' opposition to their message, we know they did so successfully: "Now when they saw the boldness of Peter and John, and perceived that they were unlearned and ignorant men, they marvelled; and they took knowledge of them, that they had been with Jesus" (Acts 4:13).

Their mimicry of Christ gave bare-faced proof that they had learned the lesson of the Model-Teacher. No other plausible explanation occurred to those priests. The ruling Sanhedrin knew all the rules of current pedagogy. They controlled access to formal education and supervised the curriculums that led to endorsement of teachers. Under their scrupulous control lay the rabbinical route to education and no one could circumvent it. They alone certified! Yet before them stood men, clearly uneducated by formal processes, who displayed demeanor, conduct, and authority that captivated the crowds. The bewildered leadership could only conclude these disciples had learned all this from their intimate relationship with Jesus. They had emulated the Exemplar!

Paul encouraged the Christians at Ephesus to be "followers of God" (Ephesians 5:1) and advised the Corinthian believers, "Be ye followers of me, even as I also am of Christ" (1 Corinthians 11:1). Paul used the Greek word, *mimetes*, from which derives the English word *mimic*. As a wise teacher, Paul modeled Christian commitment and integrity, and he sought to have the saints mimic him as he mimicked Christ. "Let us mimic the Model," he counsels.

On the night of His betrayal, the Lord Jesus assembled His disciples in the upper room and gave them the model-lesson in humility and service. No mock rehearsal or carefully staged theatrical scenario this—no closed curtains separated the awaiting audience from an actor who enraptured by show-business sleight-of-hand. This was life and death, breath-and-blood drama. The disciples would see for themselves, firsthand, what the Model-Teacher manifested. Soon Jesus would walk the solitary, soul-wrenching path to the cross. Yet according to chapter 13 of John's Gospel, after dinner, Jesus took a towel, wrapped it about Himself, poured water in a basin, and proceeded to do the dirty work of a household slave. In this hour when they, by all rights, should have catered to Him, He showed them what it meant to be servant of all. He circled the table and, one by one, he washed their grimy feet. Unhesitatingly, without fanfare or pomposity, He—Almighty God—did the dirty work! And when He finished, He asked the question: "Know ye what I have done to you?" (John 13:12). Example! When Christ, the Model-Teacher, was no longer physically present with them, they would repeat this lesson—indelibly etched on the chalkboard of their memories—which served as the basis for their own ministries.

Jesus, as Teacher, uncannily made lessons larger than life so they would retain their vividness indefinitely. For a lifetime after, each disciple would recollect this scene that agonizing night and reflect on its dramatic instruction. Christ chose situations and circumstances uniquely suited for the large, grand lessons of life and applied them to a host of more limited settings. The upper room experience was more than a localized exercise in foot washing; it gave the supreme example of selfless service. Prior to the cross, the Savior talked not about alleviating His present distress; rather, with the ease of unswerving conviction, He demonstrated the radical need for sacrifice. Lectures alone cannot communicate that; it needs to be visualized in the incarnate act of self-abnegation. Verbiage alone is vain. The task, in example, lies intertwined with the teaching.

Years later, the themes of Jesus' teaching (as evidenced in the Acts of the Apostles) are emulated and echoed in the apostles' lives. What Jesus began, the apostles continued (Acts 1:1–5). They spontaneously reflected the actions the Lord had rehearsed in their presence. But not only in service was Jesus the supreme object lesson; in sufferings, He was the paragon of patience. Peter, who knew better than most people the powerful example Jesus provided, points to the suffering Savior as our Model: "For even hereunto were ye called: because Christ also suffered for us, leaving us an example, that ye should follow in his steps" (1 Peter 2:21).

Patience and Compassion

As director of guidance for a small school district, one of my responsibilities was to monitor the special-education class, held in an old, decaying school building. The class was composed of students with disorders ranging from mild learning disabilities to emotional difficulties and the educably mentally retarded. An elderly (beyond retirement age) black teacher, whose grand-maternal affection and compassion more than compensated for the meager facilities and materials with which she had to work, cared for the class. Every weekend, two or three of the children, with their parents' permission, walked with her to the bus stop and rode the bus home with her. For those few days her home became their home.

Patience and compassion, the twin virtues of "teacherhood" adorned her presence and classroom practice. When the fatigue of bureaucratic tedium threatened to overload my emotional circuit, I retreated to her room and received refreshment as she sacrificially and uncomplainingly lived the teacher's life before her students.

If a teacher must have any one virtue, it is *patience*. My first feeble efforts in teaching had more impulsiveness than patience to them. Restraint and reserve are not easily acquired. But in Jesus, patience showed as a prominent virtue. Under the fiercest pressure, the Lord provided, in His serenity and composure, the classic illustration of patience. Abused beyond belief, He submitted to His Father, not with simple, stoic resignation, but with a nobility born of Sonship. Peter notes that the purpose for the disciples was that they would "follow in his steps." Models leave clear and irrefutable footprints as vivid and graphic maps that students can trace tangibly. As a dance instructor puts false footprints along the floor, to show the dance routine, the model-teacher creates molds into which students can step. The Lord's sandals firmly impressed His course as He strode through the hills of Galilee, along Samaria's roads, and toward Jerusalem's Temple. No one needed a magnifying glass to discover the markings: ". . . This is the way, walk ye in it . . ." (Isaiah 30:21).

Eliezer of Damascus (Genesis 15:2), the faithful steward of Abraham, was sent by his master on a mission to obtain a wife for Isaac. Eliezer prayerfully pursued the goal without the slightest deviation; he met Rebekah by the well in Nahor and brought her back with him. His assignment was clear, and he accomplished it (Genesis 24). Eliezer's commentary on this assignment and its fulfillment was: ". . . I being in the way, the Lord led me . . ." (Genesis 24:27) His specific objective precluded any error or serious mistake. Directions should be so explicit that "wayfaring men, though fools, shall not err therein" (Isaiah 35:8).

Emulating the Model

Model, a popularly used term, denotes the best or most desirable. In that sense, we are encouraged to copy the model—be copycats. As the epitome, the model embodies all the best traits and qualities. It is the essence—the *quintessence*—possessing in itself the indispensable components that define the thing in itself:

sui generis. A fashion model wears clothes in the way they should be worn, and to become this kind of model, one must have the classic composure that permits others to see the fashions in all their elegance. Medicine refers to the *model* human body, the criterion or standard by which doctors measure all medical functions. In determining illness, the model provides a consistent and unitary approach to diagnosis and evaluation. In literature, a model piece of writing allows for comparisons and reveals the defects in lesser works. The true model, therefore, encourages emulation and becomes the standard for all evaluation.

Christ, the Model-Teacher, provides the canon to which we may compare all utterances and actions. His words and works form the sole basis for making estimates about ourselves; His credentials are beyond question. We need to regulate our lives according to Him. Like cybernetics (the science of guidance and control systems), in teaching, our Lord used *feedback*. In that science, if a heating system warms a certain space some instrument must let us know whether sufficient heat gets into the space. If we wish to heat a house, we must designate a desired temperature; whenever conditions deviate from the specified "comfort range," adjustment becomes necessary. Although the heating unit provides heat, something else must tell how much heat is needed. Hence, the system has a thermostat that monitors and feeds back any departure from acceptable limits. When the limits are trespassed, the thermostat triggers the heating apparatus. As a result of that feedback, the system alters its operations and regulates activity.

Viewed as our Exemplar, the Lord Jesus provides the perfect pattern for our lives. His life, love, and language feed back into our spiritual systems, and we adjust as we see our lives "out of sync" with Him. Using His life as the grand design, we trace the pattern of our lives. If we seek *only* to emulate those about us, we will, invariably, incorporate the defects of their lives into ours. When this tracing of other people becomes the dominant practice, each generation of disciples will grow farther and farther away from the true Type of Christ. The prototypic pattern of Jesus will soon be replaced with cheap, defective copies, and the result will not resemble the original.

We need human models, of course. We will seek to pattern our lives after paragons and produce in ourselves the best of others, who *inspire* us to *aspire*. But we Christians must exercise caution because we can also unwittingly copy ill-considered and harmful practices. We dare not be like Prospero's pupil, Caliban, in William Shakespeare's *The Tempest*, who confessed: "You taught me language; and my profit on't Is, I know how to curse." All pupils must be cast in the mold of the Model-Teacher and they should "represent" Him.

The great teachers in all times have been examples for students to follow. For significant learning to occur, students have to identify with their teachers. Unless they see the teacher as a mirror that reflects potential for growth, few students will respond. On an end-of-the-course evaluation sheet I read the frightening and flattering comment of a student who said he wanted to be like me! Particularly, he had been inspired to enrich his own vocabulary because he liked my "way with words."

All great teachers have given testimony to the influence of a model-teacher in their lives. John Dewey was influenced by the "yankee schoolmaster" William T. Harris, and Professor H. A. Torrey "turned his thoughts to the study of philosophy as a life pursuit."[9] Greatness cannot come without contact with someone who is great. Greatness is gleaned just as mediocrity is mimicked. Shoddiness breeds shoddiness. Perhaps the proliferation of second-rate models, whether in education or other areas of social life, has producd the shabby culture some commentators contend exists today. One man's dismal description reads like this:

> The puzzle is why so many people live so badly. Not so wickedly but so inanely. Not so cruelly, but so stupidly. There is little to admire and less to imitate in the people who are prominent in our culture. We have celebrities not saints. Famous entertainers amuse a nation of bored insomniacs. Infamous criminals act out the aggressions of timid conformists. Petulant and spoiled athletes play games vicariously for lazy and apathetic spectators. People, aimless and bored, amuse

themselves with trivia and trash. Neither the adventure of goodness nor the pursuit of righteousness gets headlines.[10]

We can never rise to greater heights than the ones we see. Someone has to see beyond the horizon and show us that something more exists than this speck of a world in which we live. On two separate occasions, Jesus, having come down from the mountain (of the Beatitudes and the Transfiguration) was accosted by the crowds. In each instance, people pressed their needs upon Him. Having declared the kingdom principles, He began to implement them. By explication and *example*, He inaugurated the redemptive plan on the sea level of life's common plain. His disciples learned by hearing and *doing*. The combination of these vital aspects of teaching served to facilitate learning. Pronouncement cannot divorce itself from practice. John Dewey, the father of Progressive Education, coined the term "learning by doing,"[11] but unlike his misguided followers who trivialized the idea by reducing it to random activity, Dewey prescribed actions explicitly related to objectives.

Our Lord intervened in lives. In all that He did in life's rugged reality, Jesus was not only *an* example, He was *the* Exemplar. Not only did He demonstrate what we must do, He showed the *way* in which we need to do it. Things worth doing are worth doing in a *worthy* manner. The most sublime duty, done in a slipshod way, simply becomes an exercise in shoddiness.

The Quest for Excellence

The ancient Greeks employed a term to express this quest for excellence—*arete*. The word does not translate well into English. Full of shades and subtleties English does not suggest, *arete* ranges in meaning from "virtue" to "valor," but the idea of striving toward excellence remains implicit in it. E. B. Castle, in his study of ancient education, defines it this way: "*Arete* was the peculiar excellence that makes a thing . . . the best, the most effective of [its] kind. . . . there emerges a new idea of human worth in the character that unites nobility of action with nobility of man."[12]

The word *arete* modified in meaning as the Greeks increasingly refined the concept of excellence and no longer limited expectations for excellence to simple physical prowess. H. I. Marrou's classic treatment of ancient education provides a historical development of the definition of the term.[13] Initially, *arete* meant "valor in the chivaloric sense—the quality of the brave man, the hero." Eventually, accompanying a "moral revolution," it took on the meaning of something other than sheer physical conquest. It acquired a refinement that suggested something spiritual in nature, which would transcend the accomplishment of the present and leave a legacy for generations. *Arete* then undergoes a qualitative transformation, as defined by Socrates, and is now imbued with love: "It involved an aspiration towards a higher perfection, an ideal of excellence. . . ."[14] The concept of *arete* (excellence) and *paideia* (education) become linked together by *agape* (love). The progression continues until *arete* leads to awareness of submission as the means to truth (*aletheia*). As *arete* is elevated to a more lofty stage the element of arrogance that permeated earlier efforts toward *arete* are purged: ". . . It is by Truth and not by power-techniques that he will lead his pupil to *arete*, to spiritual perfection, to virtue: the ultimate aim of human education is achieved by submitting to the demands of the Absolute."[15]

The model-teacher provides the living linkage between *arete* and *agape*. Did not the apostle proclaim the "more excellent way" through love? ". . . And yet I show you a more excellent way. Though I speak with the tongues of men and of angels, and have not charity. . . . I am nothing" (1 Corinthians 12:31; 13:1, 2). As we watch, with fixed gaze, the motions of the Master-Teacher, we see love in action. What the ancients quested for, we see incarnated and exemplified in the person of our Lord Jesus Christ: the Pattern, the Paragon, the Exemplar, the Model-Teacher.

10
ENLARGING
THE MYSTERY

. . . Great is the mystery of godliness. . . .

1 Timothy 3:16

. . . And these I see, these sparkling eyes, these stores of mystic meaning. . . .[1]

He is a sorry teacher who shows the merely obvious. Jesus enlarged the mystery.[2]

> *In this house with starry dome,*
> *Floored with gem-like plains and seas,*
> *Shall I never feel at home,*
> *Never wholly be at ease?*[3]

The term *mystic* has fallen on hard times. Images of doe-eyed, sexless, seraphic beings enveloped in ethereal light seem to surface when we use that word. But I have seen them—rare as they are—they do exist and do not resemble the caricature we have drawn of them. They move with a freedom that the base and too earthbound never know, liberated from preoccupation with their own performance and the paranoia it brings.

I recall a clear image: junior-year high-school geometry class. Faded, unglossed chalkboards. Dome lights heavy with accretions of lifeless insects. Aged floorboards that creaked, and unventilated air that hung heavy in the room. When the teacher walked in, the room became bathed in a sacramental ambience. You could almost touch the change. His deportment — his carriage was charged with a gentle current of charisma. He was neither flamboyant nor flaccid. Quiet dignity, but not stiff indifference. Students felt magnetically attracted to him; they wanted to be around that kind of teacher. He captivated without enslaving; he smiled without the inanity of the clown. Other teachers would move quietly to the side when he walked down the hallway, and his personal processional would pass through. He never sought an entourage, but it followed wherever he went — the envy of the other faculty.

Reviving the Mystery

Schools today seem to hold so little mystery. Our penchant for the clearly rational and our apotheosis of logic have robbed education of its enchantment. Neither C. S. Lewis's nor J. R. R. Tolkien's creation of Lilliputian worlds of sweet, magical enchantments detracted from their scholarly credibility; perhaps this quality of enchantment enhanced their awareness in other areas of academia. Today's disenchanted society, with its predictable control obsession leaves little room for wonder. All too early, the harsh reality of a technological world assaults children's minds, factoring out the magic education should supply. We leave no room in the curriculum for whimsy. If only we could rediscover Tennyson's sense of delicate magic as he contemplated the charm and enigma of a common flower:

> *Flower in the crannied wall,*
> *I pluck you out of the crannies;—*
> *I hold you here, root and all, in my hand,*
> *Little flower—but if I could understand*
> *What you are, root and all, and all in all,*
> *I should know what God and man is.*[4]

Charles Edward Garman, teacher of philosophy at Amherst College, doubtless possessed the charm that put him among the mystic-teachers. One of his students recalled when Garman, to illustrate a philosophical point, quoted Tennyson's poem:

> I shall never forget the day he recited Tennyson's Flower in the Crannied Wall. It was like listening to the voice of an oracle. . . . Garman's attitude toward his students was peculiar, as was their reaction to it. To many he remained ever remote, even mystical. . . . In various ways, he impressed the intellectual, the religious, the shy, the sceptical, the frivolous. . . . He possessed dignity with the grace of humor, and the salt of speech.[5]

For the mystic-teacher, the classroom is not an aseptic environment where "neither germs nor genius grows." In its pixie world, patterns change and reshape quickly, without fear; enchantment and ecstasy are not incompatible with learning in this place. George Leonard, attuned to the mystic-teacher's style and working space, describes it: "A classroom, any classroom is an awesome place of shadows and shifting colors, a place of unacknowledged desires and unnamed powers, a magic place."[6]

The mystic-teacher knows, as William I. Thompson says, that the schoolhouse is a "universe . . . not made out of matter but out of music."[7] A lyrical quality permeates the mystic-teacher's space. Precise, linear measurements give way to varied, geodesic space, and configurations rearrange themselves constantly in this educational place of encounter. The mystic-teacher is not boxed in by rectangular thinking. Her right brain frees up the metaphysical, and she thinks mosaically. The linear, sequential programming of the brain's left hemisphere does not tyrannize the mystic-teacher.

Logic *is* necessary in an ordered world. Science can take us beyond ourselves, with its extension of the senses, so that we can peer and probe and move beyond the borders of unaided eyes and ears. But only the mystic-teacher can cause our spirits to move from the earthbound gravitational pull of the world of sensation. Spirits and souls define us more fully than do our bodies.

Secret Places of the Soul

Jesus Christ, the Mystic-Teacher, shows us that God "is to be sought and found in the secret places of the soul." In the final outcome we cannot discover reality in the material. In part, education will provide us with tools and techniques to handle the world of molecules and milliseconds—of time and toil—but we dare not settle for this as the sum total of all education or confuse it with learning's perfect purpose. Jesus was not a tradesman teaching His students a saleable skill. Had He proposed this as His appointed task, He would have gathered the disciples about Him in the carpenter's shop in Nazareth. In the wonder of the inner sanctuary lurk the unsuspected yearnings toward greatness and Godlikeness. "The mystic's finger is on the skirts of God. . . ."[8] Jesus was a stranger in this world, although He made His home in it. A holy dissatisfaction—a sense of being ill-at-ease with its style and conduct—remained with Him.

Malcolm Muggeridge, a mystic in his own right, claimed a similar lack of kinship with this world; and he confessed himself a stranger to its order.[9]

The teacher who becomes too at home with the taken-for-granted priorities in modern education seldom moves students to grasp the wonder of God or of their own existence. A sense of self-consciousness, coupled with self-abasement, envelops the mystic-teacher. For him the world of sensation never sets the limits or levels of aspiration. Her piercing vision sees through to the other side. Such teachers have "poetic" penetration and see life in mosaics rather than in rigid forms. Truth lies beyond the fact. Meaning is more than the simple experience, and as T. S. Eliot noted, the nonmystical may have the experience but miss the meaning.

Myth provides the filter through which truth is filtered for the mystic. The mystic-teacher conceives of life in its mythical grandeur—myth in this case being defined by C. S. Lewis and others not as the denial of historical fact but the larger awareness of its truth and interpretation. The "whole" is more than the "sum of its parts," to use the gestaltist's phrase.

The distinction C. S. Lewis makes between the *phenomenal* and the *noumenal* is partly the difference between the realms in which the mystic and nonmystic teachers move.[10] The mystic-teacher is aware of and attentive to the *noumenal*—that powerful, pervading presence of transcendence. The Lord Jesus was always within that realm—the shekinah glory of God testified to the eternal noumena (Exodus 13:21, 22; Matthew 17:5).

During the 1960s and early 1970s, students revolted in society and on campuses, in part because of their disenchantment with the excessive technology and rationality of a whimsyless world. The Newtonian clock world of regularity and monotonous sameness, imposed upon an educational and social order, stifled the human spirit. There were no longer any flights of fancy. All travel was done on respectable, technology-provided modes of transportation. With no suitable mode for the soul available, it remained wingless. The soul's true realm is in the transcendence of God's truth, but B. F. Skinner and his new breed of behaviorists debunked the notion of "autonomous man," and routinized everything. Formulas began to replace inner explanations. Ironically, in the early 1970s, along came *Jonathan Livingston Seagull* and soared, not above into the outer world of space, but into the inner world of quasi-mystical self. This was one bold attempt to break the slavish hold of machines on man's soul.

"In the largest sense, what the students seem to be against was the entire value system of our present, technological civilization . . . the realm of the external and stultifying. What they seemed to be for was an entirely different value system which we could call, perhaps, aesthetic, or noumenal or maybe even religious. But perhaps the best word would be mythic. . . ."[11]

As the Mystic-Teacher, Christ filled the longings of man. He taught not about the religion of rites and obsolete rituals, but the religion of ultimate relationship: "This is life eternal, that they might know thee the only true God, and Jesus Christ, whom thou hast sent" (John 17:3). George Morrison reminds us that the "one great service which mysticism renders is to keep religion from rigidity."[12] Education today has a crying need for Christian mysticism: "It is God's corrective for that intense activity which is so characteristic of the modern church" and school.[13]

Transcendence or Technique?

A mystic-teacher's distinctive attribute is his constant orientation toward the transcendent. The eternal reference point (which Jean Paul Sartre futilely sought and never found) does not evade him. Never will he leave students clinging hopelessly to fragments of shifting sensation in the turbulence of contemporary education. She will always talk about God, even if she is not allowed! I feel thankful for the fearless few who never hesitated to teach me about God. Certainly in Sunday school I learned at least that much from them. Some were matronly women who knew God, but carefully kept a discreet distance. Others, more maternal, effused spiritual care. Among them, stands out a lady (in the finest sense of the term) who taught me about God. She was young and the pastor's wife. Sunday mornings were times and Sunday schools were places where she in an unaffected manner talked about our heavenly Father. I was glad to know someone like this God existed. Spontaneous and warm, our teacher never ignored the reality of our harsh and prospectless lives. She never denied the bitterness of life's sullied streams from which the youngsters in that class drank each day. But she also never left us there. If we could not go to God, she quite naturally brought God to us. Who would have guessed in those days, which proved golden, that in a few short years, our Sunday-school teacher and her pastor-husband would move to Europe and establish the international ministry of L'Abri, in Switzerland. The Schaeffers would become household names for a generation of searchers for truth and seekers for God. Edith Schaeffer served as a committed Sunday-school teacher before she became a celebrated author and Christian celebrity.[14]

Education today too eagerly defines teachers as technicians. Increasingly, curriculums in schools are designed simply to provide students with saleable skills to serve a consumption society. With one prospective college student and her parents I discussed the possibilities of the majors she could take in college and the options available. The student felt interested in pursuing a career in music, but her parents tried to discourage her.

"What can you do with music?" the mother kept asking. "There's no money in music, and career opportunities are limited. Why don't you consider computers or a program in business?"

The daughter's face dropped. I could tell she did not relish the prospect of sitting before a computer terminal, reading interminable printouts. I explained to the parents that for a Christian, higher education should be foremost and fundamentally the opportunity to increase and enhance options for Christ's service. Higher education, I said, involved stewardship, and we should allow God's leading and submit to it, irrespective of the potential payoff. We dare not calculate everything, educationally, in terms of the commercial and economic outcomes.

Jacques Ellul, the contemporary critic of excessive technology, indicts the education that emphasizes consumerism and makes students pawns in the hands of a capricious and tyrannical technological ogre. Students who opt for education solely because of the technical skills, says Ellul: " . . . Will be the servants, the most conformable imaginable, of the instruments of technique. . . . And education will no longer be an unpredictable and exciting adventure in human enlightenment, but an exercise in conformity and an apprenticeship to whatever gadgetry is useful in a technical world."[15]

I explained to that student's parents that my own daughter was pursuing a career in music, because she liked music and had developed ability. I had no naively optimistic ideas about the vocational opportunities in her field. I knew it was highly competitive and limited; nevertheless, I saw the value for her as a person to pursue that area of interest. "The world never has too much music," I told them. We need to develop God-given talents in stewardship, and when people sing or play or compose with that in mind, they do not then pollute or desecrate.

The Lord Jesus radiated a mystical aura. Doubtless, His deity was its source, but in His clear, transparent humanity, He attracted people to Himself. Fishermen followed Him; Matthew abandoned a lucrative life-style and went with Him; women from Galilee followed closely and ministered from their personal wealth. All who numbered themselves as His disciples knew that among them was the "mystical Headship of Christ" and they were in "mystical union of Christ with each individual believer and each individual believer's mystical union with Christ."[16]

The mystic-teacher is not the impractical spinner of abstractions we have imagined. "The mystic too full of God to speak intelligibly to the world," is not true of Christ. Paul, the mighty apostle of sweet mystical visions, who talks about the unmeasurable dimensions of God's love (Ephesians 3:18, 19), shows himself, above all men, "a man of vigor, vitality and concrete practicality." The mystics A. W. Tozer was fond of and whose writings he read voraciously were saints who sanctified the ordinary, and where they walked, footprints became halos.[17]

The Essential Renewal

The life of every effective teacher requires times apart from the routine of life for restoration and renewal; teachers continually involved in the lives of students can never sustain a successful teaching career. Quiet times come not just for devotional life, but for professional growth. In silence, "far from the madding crowd," apart from the din of incessant demands, one develops mystical insights. Jesus sought renewal of energy in mystic communion with the Father. After three days of uninterrupted teaching, the Lord sent the multitudes back to their homes and hamlets. He did not hesitate to hang the DO NOT DISTURB sign on His door.

But mysticism is something more than that if we take it in its religious sense. It is the doctrine that God is to be sought and found in the secret place of the soul. Not in the outward world, however beautiful, is the true vision of God to be attained. Sunrise and sunset and the evening—these are but the outskirts of His ways. It is in the soul within us, in the hidden sanctuary, in the silence and secret of the human heart that the union which is true blessedness is won and the vision is granted which is peace. For this end, says the mystic, must a man learn to withdraw into himself. He must learn to practice, whatever pain it costs him, the spiritual method of detachment . . . and so, in silence and alone and self-absorbed, shall he awaken to the fact of God.[18]

All the great teachers of God's Word—the ones whose works and words echo down to this day—press upon us this key to teaching effectiveness and power. In the splendor of personal silence, we cultivate the quiet sense of mystic renewal as the Spirit alone communicates. The Spirit cannot be heard by a cacophonous age.

Earlier in my career, my office door was *always* open, and the traffic never stopped. I enjoyed the conversation and student interaction. But soon each day would dwindle to its close, and I found myself fatigued and crowded in by stacks of unattended to and unmarked papers. The treadmill of personal involvement tires, even as it gets us nowhere. Teachers, I had naively and ill-informedly assumed, were always available. I felt guilty when I closed the door, but I have learned that in essential hiatuses of reflection and meditation, I restore myself in communion with God. No teacher can be a prophet to his own age unless He listens to the voice of God, and teachers must be prophets to their generation as David was to his (Acts 13:36). Each classroom is a forum where the issues of life must be proclaimed with integrity. The dearth of mystics among us witnesses to the anemia in education.

I feel thankful for college professors who addressed the eternal verities in the context of everyday concerns, spontaneously acknowledging God's working in all of life. They did not labor or lumber about, trying to effect some artificial integration of faith and learning. Their mystical sense of transcendence was unforced and apparent. Like Garman of Amherst, they had this special sense: "He was mysterious to those of us who sat daily in his classroom listening to his strangely resonant voice, watching his hypnotic eyes. . . . There was something of the mystic about him, something of the prophet and seer."[19]

Garman was in touch with deity. He published no books, had limited visibility in the world outside Amherst College, and seldom occupied a platform or pulpit, but William James described him as "the greatest teacher."

The teachers that touched me most and imparted mystical awareness were for the most part in philosophy and literature and occasionally in an education class. My first encounter with Shakespeare took place in high school, with a brooding, melancholic teacher—a modern Hamlet of sorts. A distant look dwelt in his eyes, and at times a curious expression crossed his face; then it seemed that for a brief second he had journeyed to another world and left the class alone. But quickly he returned and uttered stirring words. I had never before known such presence in any class. I enjoyed the comic teachers (and the school had its share).

I knew all the pundits and pontificators. I sat in awe of the
erudite, with their endless knowledge. Other teachers, world
travelers, kept us spellbound with their tales of lands and scenes.
But this one, with the modesty so typical of mystics, would quote
endlessly from *Hamlet* or *MacBeth* or *King Lear*.

The Divine Spark

Mystic-teachers work from the inside out. They take riddles
and unravel them. They spin delicate images from words, the
way a spider weaves its intricate web. A calm, unhurried pace
accompanies their presence. A vision—an inner vision—guides
them. The mystic-teacher in my literature class said with
softness: " 'To be or not to be.' The essence of life and eternity
is in that infinitive. Everything reduces itself to those six
words." "The Hamletian query," he called it, "the most
succinct statement of all the urgings that eternity has placed
within us. The existential encounter . . . the cutting edge of
being and nonbeing. Do we dare to choose our way—do we dare
to 'take arms against a sea of troubles' or do we, like 'the quarry
slave' capitulate to cowardice and slither into the hole of
acquiescence?" Bit by bit, with a magic wand of imagery, he
unveiled the possibilities in a piece of poetry. "He almost
seemed to be to the more devoted of his disciples as if the divine
spark within him had been fanned to such a heat that, . . . it was
burning him up. He lived and died, indeed, for a vision, and the
ecstasy of it was in those eyes."[20]

Our Lord was not a mere technician in His teaching; His method
never became merely mechanical. He took His hearers to the
point of ecstasy. He took them outside themselves (Greek:
ekstasis). He turned His disciples inside out, and they in turn
turned their world upside down (Acts 17:6). By His teaching He
created joy—the kind of joy C. S. Lewis pursued and found in his
own experience.[21] The Mystic-Teacher makes education ecstatic.

What great appeal did Christ have for the masses (which,
conversely, gained the enmity of His enemies)? It was His inner
dynamic, which manifested itself in His personal mystique. No

man could explain His teachings simply on the basis of the traditional, "conventional wisdom." His words found their lodging within the inner being, just as they came from within His inner being. Calvin sees the relationship in its rightful order: "It is Christ, the interior teacher, who will teach us. It is He who causes men to give external signs in order that, turning inwardly to Him, we may receive His lessons."[22]

The undiscerning have accused Jesus of being a starry-eyed dreamer who ignored life's realities. "An impractical, simple-minded man," some would say. "It would be better if He took His naive ideas to some type of Disney World." That's the same charge his brothers brought against Joseph; "this dreamer," they called him (Genesis 37:19). But that dreamer kept a nation from starvation. Mystical Joseph, soul always open to the mysterious, took on the sophisticated society of Egypt, on its own terms and beat it at its own game. "Joseph dreamed a dream . . . and they hated him yet the more" (Genesis 37:5). But soon Pharaoh elevated him to premier of the land.

Jesus and all the mystic-teachers who follow after Him dream dreams. They dare to see beyond the surface.

> Our art teacher . . . was a painter with a poetic soul. Mystical and idiosyncratic in his art, he was real and direct in life. We thrived on this vital contrast. Most teachers warned us to face reality . . . [he] endowed us with a sense of mystery. . . .[23]

> Our history teacher had a magic touch. His classes set our minds on fire. We emerged from them as if from a dream. He understood our longings . . . and led us into a labyrinth of legends, myths, and mysteries. . . . The specific and the symbolic emerged with clarity.[24]

The visionaries are the mystics, and they teach with vision. With William Blake they share the poetic awareness of the world beyond worlds and the world within lives:

To see a World in a Grain of Sand
and a Heaven in a Wild Flower
Hold Infinity in the palm of your hand
and eternity in an hour.[25]

Mystic-teachers see *"through* the eye," not *with* the eye. Malcolm Muggeridge, taking his lead from Blake, knows that the organs of sense alone tell us nothing of other worlds, and the mystic-teacher with a romantic impulse will penetrate the commonplace of "flesh and substance" and see clear through to the other side.[26] The fourth dimension unfolds, with its valley of the vision of angels (as Elisha showed the young man in 2 Kings 6:17), when we see through the eye. Paul saw the mystical revelation of Jesus when his companions saw nothing (Acts 9:7). At the tomb of Lazarus, the mourners saw a corpse; Jesus saw the glory of God (John 11:4). When in the midst of the storm, the disciples rowed feverishly, frightened by the turbulence, the mystic figure walked calmly upon the disturbed sea and in a voice of sublime control whispered: "Be of good cheer: it is I; be not afraid" (Mark 6:50).

As when a storm is raging on the sea, and in that storm is some one whom we love . . . we are no longer fearful, but can look across the crested waters and be still, so when once out of the stormy sea we have drawn Christ into the secret place, then for us there is no terror in the tempest. . . . There is Christ arising . . . mysterious, ineffable, sublime. . . .[27]

— Part III —
THE MASTER
AS TEACHER

In His teachings, during that ministry on earth, the Master combined the mystic and the practical in a way no other teacher has before or since. A look at the Master's ways will prove profitable for all aspiring master-teachers. Above all other lessons His is the message that never dies.

11
THE MASTER-
TEACHER

. . . We know that thou art a teacher come from God. . . .

John 3:2

In private conversation, he had a mastery of words, a voice, a vigor, a freedom, a dignity, and therefore what one might call an authority in which he stood quite alone.[1]

Christ was a great teacher because He created great people out of the people as colorless and with as little promise as your people here. . . . That must be your standard . . . for teaching these children. . . . If you would be a great teacher, you must never let go the idea that greatness is the rule and character of the human race, not the exception.[2]

Horror stories of the compromised position of the educational enterprise in the United States fill the popular press and professional periodicals. In 1982, the United States Department of Education published its alarming report, *A Nation at Risk,* which declared: "Our nation is at risk. Our once unchallenged preeminence . . . is being overtaken by competitors throughout the world. . . . What was unimaginable a generation ago has begun to occur—others are matching and surpassing our educational attainments."[3]

This country has been plunged into paranoia over the deterioration of teaching and the qualifications of teachers. The National Commission on Excellence in Education cried out for educational reform and recommended that we recruit more academically able students into the teacher ranks and that master-teachers design preparation programs and school curricula.

Excellence has become the rallying cry in contemporary education; merit replaces mediocrity. In the highly competitive climate of modern schooling, teachers who demonstrate instructional competency, mastery of subject matter, and superior communication skills receive preference. The concept of the "master-teacher" has emerged as the most significant factor in shaping the present approach to teacher education. Prompted in part by the perilous condition into which education has presumably fallen, emphasis upon demonstrated instructional mastery has increased.

The Master-Teacher

The *Nation at Risk* report has become the imperative for school reform and the mandate for the identification and development of a corps of master-teachers. The seemingly antiquated notion of the "schoolmaster" has been revived, and clear guidelines have been established for the identification of master-teachers. Benjamin Bloom of the University of Chicago has suggested five key criteria for identifying such individuals:

1. Superior knowledge of the subject
2. Skill in teaching
3. Command respect of students
4. Constantly nurturing the students in the subject
5. Produce demonstrable results[4]

No longer will society contentedly accept inadequately qualified classroom mannequins who masquerade as teachers. Educational authorities have demanded that each classroom be under the control of a master-teacher. Invariably, students who have distinguished themselves in academic and professional pursuits attribute their success to teachers who have demonstrated superior knowledge and skills and who have motivated their students to high levels of accomplishment. These exceptional teachers possess the vital pairing of scholarship and sensitivity and have earned an "almost reverential respect" from their students.

Master-teachers manifest all the elements Bloom identified. They are the originators and innovators, setting the pace for other teachers. Their superiority, however, is not simply limited to technical expertise. They "must have an analytical awareness of what they do to be effective and also know how to communicate this awareness. . . ."[5] They create the molds from which other teachers will be cast. They possess an intuitive awareness of the proper thing to do in the classroom. John Dewey has said that "they are masters precisely because they do not follow either models or rules but subdue both of these things to serve enlargement of personal experience."[6]

As the concept of master-teacher gains popularity in current educational practice, career ladders encourage advancement up the educational rungs. Through discipline and demonstrated competency, the master-teacher emerges and shares knowledge with other teachers. Some 2,400 years ago, Plato identified his own criteria to select his master-teacher—the philosopher-king. He must demonstrate:

> . . . A constant passion for any knowledge that will reveal . . . something of the reality which endures forever and is not always passing into and out of existence. . . . [this] desire is to know the whole of that reality. . . . Another trait which the nature we are seeking cannot fail to possess—truthfulness, a love of truth, and a hatred of falsehood that will not tolerate untruth in any form. . . . Hence, besides our other requirements, we shall look for a mind endowed with measure and grace, which will be instinctively drawn to see every reality in its true light.[7]

Through a series of progressively rigorous requirements, students advance in education, and after diligent study, arrive at successively higher levels of learning. A select few who have shown their superiority can aspire to the title of master-teacher. Having ascended to the pedagogical pinnacle, through study and self-mastery, they are equipped to instruct.

Sent to Teach

A good teacher is a Godsend. Many teachers *come* into our lives, but only the master-teachers are *sent*. Reflecting upon our school years, we can all remember a few teachers who have left us different from the way they found us. In that vague parade of faces that marched through classrooms and jostled us in corridors, many of whom remain shadowy figures, one or two monumental people touched our lives with special mastery and imparted purpose. We meandered through the academic maze, at times not quite certain what it was all about. Prescribed programs were routinely followed. Someday, our teachers told us, it would all fit together, but we doubted that. The disconnected series of hollow experiences in hallowed halls never quite seemed to link together. But serendipity, in the form of a teacher, caught us unaware and surprised us into self-realization. The charm of teachers who transformed our banal schooldays and refreshed us told us God had sent them.

We had our fill of the "perfunctory professoriat." Like vending machines, they dispensed knowledge on cue. Like the sophists of ancient Greece, who peddled their wares in the academic marketplaces, today's self-styled specialists have answers to all but the most important questions: ". . . The sophists dazzled everyone without convincing anyone of anything positive. . . . they argued unsystematically and unfairly, but painted over the gaps in their reasoning with glossy rhetoric. . . . they had few constructive ideas. . . . they demonstrated that almost anything could be proved by a fast talker. . . . They never allowed anyone else to get a word in edgewise."[8]

They set up shop and cater to the consumer mentality. Their premise: anything for a price. They parcel out people in piecemeal fashion, without concern for soul or spirit. With their expertise and closely guarded areas of specialty, they claim mastership of their craft but in fact, merely manipulate others. Sadly, in every age, some disgrace the sacred title of *teacher,* and schools may produce "products," skilled and adept in their scholarly disciplines, but lacking human compassion. In Haim Ginott's book *Teacher and Child* a school principal who had been the victim of human brutality offered this caveat to his teachers:

> Dear teacher:
> I am the survivor of a concentration camp. My eyes saw what no man should witness:
> Gas chambers built by *learned* engineers.
> Children poisoned by *educated* physicians.
> Infants killed by *trained* nurses.
> Women and babies shot and burned by *high school* and *college* graduates.
> So, I am suspicious of education. My request is: Help your students become human. Your efforts must never produce learned monsters, skilled psychopaths, educated Eichmanns.

Reading, writing, arithmetic are important only if they serve to make our children more humane.[9]

The Mastered Teachers

Master-teachers are so named because they have been mastered. Unlike technicians, who open their bag of tricks and play pedagogic games, true teachers reveal truth—and essentially reveal themselves. Students know they're "for real." Having gained sufficient strength to risk putting themselves on the line, master-teachers transmit that to their students. Good teachers are repositories of strength, which they have gained over years of experience; the weak teacher lacks the depth of experience that builds it. I recall one ineffective, unimaginative teacher who boasted to the entire faculty that she had thirty years of teaching experience. A colleague retorted: "You've had one year of experience thirty times!"

We call teaching a "helping profession," and through self-disclosure the strong teacher helps and empowers students. But the master-teacher has gained power through submission, an unbreakable foundation. Paul, the master builder, reminds us that in construction we build on strength alone. Likewise, without a stable and secure educational foundation, the superstructure we build will come crashing down (1 Corinthians 3:11–15)

Ancient Mastered Teachers

The finest and fullest expression of Western education developed in the classical period of ancient Greece. Socrates, Plato, and Aristotle form the teacher triumvirate unsurpassed for inquiry into wisdom. The teaching style of Socrates was largely "inquisitional." A good question was more valuable than wealth. In gadfly fashion, Socrates probed for truth and upset tradition in the process. Unafraid to confess ignorance, he challenged the "know-it-alls" who supported the status quo, with its injustice and inequity. In a sense Socrates had submitted, accepting his own lack of knowledge. Censored by his society, he was forced to drink the cup of hemlock; but before his death, he recruited the illustrious follower Plato. Plato then established the Academy, at Athens, and in his *Dialogues* lionized the mentor to whom he had submitted for a time. A master-teacher, Plato systematized the human quest for wisdom, and now, as British scholar A. N. Whitehead has noted, all philosophy is but a footnote to Plato.

In turn, Plato bequeathed this legacy of learning to Aristotle, who arrived at the Academy at the age of fourteen. After years of teaching and intense inquiry, Plato looked about to find that all his students had gone—except Aristotle, who remained with the master for more than two decades and became, himself, a master-teacher. The divisions and categories of knowledge in schools today can trace their origins to the teaching of Aristotle, and the university system that emerged in the Middle Ages established its curricula on the seven liberal arts he originated.

Jesus the Mastered Teacher

The Lord Jesus Christ the Master-Teacher par excellence, "Moved with perfect ease of conscious mastery."[10] He moved among men and astonished them with His life and teaching. Having submitted to the mastery of God the Father, He came not to do His own will, but the will of God, who sent Him (John 5:30). He excited the crowd's attention and earned His disciples' admiration by the personal mastery that controlled and emanated from Him; it hallmarked His ministry. Unlike the scribes and Pharisees, He did not reduce His teaching to an insipid cookbook approach or cloud it with undecipherable esoteric jargon. He spoke with accuracy and authority. His audiences, accustomed to the authoritarianism that pervaded the Roman society, reinforced by power and coercion, had seen so little authority that flowed from the person. But now the Christ—the charismatic Christ[11]—came among them, possessing an inner dynamism that manifested itself in the words He spoke and the ways He taught.

Clear of Purpose

Throughout the Gospel accounts, our Lord moved with the mastery of One who possessed a sense of unimpeded, divine purpose. Only the teacher linked with the ultimate reality of life will impress his hearers and convince his inquirers. The pedagogue who halts between two opinions, unable to make up his mind on any issue (1 Kings 18:21), is incapable of a sound and solid stance. Hopping and hedging are not conducive to credibility. People search for knowledge and desperately seek incontrovertible truth; equivocation alienates students. At some point in the lesson the teacher must declare truth. Like politics, education has become guilty of the "doublespeak" that characterized George Orwell's demogogic society of *1984*.[12] When few speak with clarity, the teacher who dispels the verbal fog and illumines the life of the students will never lack an audience.

Jesus Christ walks and talks with the authority born of divine purpose. Whether along the seashore or atop the summit, His steps are surefooted and His speech straightforward. His mastery is derived from His majesty. In the Gospel of Matthew, the Master-Teacher captivates the crowds and attracts the multitudes with His kingly presence. Clear, unmuddled purpose motivates Him as He ascends alone the ridge against the flow of the crowd who move in a downward direction. His firm footprints upon the sands mark out the unaltered course He follows, and along its circumscribed route, He meets people whom He will enlist as students in His school of discipleship. Searching for the teachable ones, He finds them already at work. He will redirect this initiative and energy into more productive paths and will channel fishing skills toward eternal purposes. It is not the idle whom the Lord summons—leisurely perhaps, but never lazy. His pace is unhurried but His approach is unhindered. The Teacher-King seeks those who willingly lean to learn. Arrogance always alienates. Mastery of any subject or specialty requires the subordination of "self." Meekness must precede mastery and is prerequisite for the ones who would learn of Him (Matthew 11:29). John the

Baptist's maxim must ever remain the student's mandate: "He must increase, but I must decrease" (John 3:30). Ter Tersteegen puts it poetically and powerfully:

> *To learn and yet to learn*
> *Whilst life goes by;*
> *So pass the student's days.*
> *And thus be great*
> *And do great things and die,*
> *And lie embalmed with praise.*
>
> *My work is but to lose and to forget*
> *Thus small despised to be.*
> *All to unlearn, this task before me set,*
> *Unlearn all else but Thee.*[13]

The eternal Son of God actively submitted to the will of His Father. Not by assertion and arrogant displays of divine prerogatives did he gain mastery over all, but by humble acquiescence to His Father's predetermined design. During the silent years in Nazareth, times of solitude when strength worked its ways within Him, "Jesus increased . . ." (Luke 2:52). Self-imposed anonymity was the precondition for recognition of His mastery. Only in uncluttered settings can maturity develop. Distractions and disturbances dissipate energy and do not permit the inner life to flourish, while seasons of solitude and undisturbed solace allow inner connections to develop.

Parker Palmer, a college professor, discovered a kind of teaching developed by Abba Felix, during the fourth century A.D. when education was formed around a monastic model that allowed considerable time for contemplation. In the monastic mode, words, which we may lose or render redundant by excessive use, can become revived and regenerated. Palmer confessed that in his own college teaching experience, "There came a time of dryness when I found it difficult to meet my classes, to speak in public . . . convinced that conditions in the academy had caused my words to dry up." The life of mind and spirit may wilt before the blast of harsh breath. Without fresh inhalations, speech becomes stale.[14]

Jesus would not make a hasty or hurried move before the optimum time for His ministry. As the Master, Jesus instructed His disciples in the importance of the right time, and they learned in their own element. Christ never retired to the "ivory tower" of aloofness, behind closed doors or within cloistered walls, once His time for public instruction had come. He enjoyed refreshing interludes, but never a permanent retreat. The Master-Teacher walked about in the real world of men and mud, where most people live: He waded in the sea, where laboring men caught the fish; He strode along the seashore, where He taught people; He lived with toil and trial. With fishermen, He launched into the deep, and they learned the lesson that He was Master of the depths. The common people heard Him gladly, because He always stayed within earshot. He ate in their houses and welcomed their hospitality.

Available to Students

Among many religions of the world, seldom is the master so accessible. Eastern mystics often live in "splendid isolation," and adherents to the faith must travel long distances for an audience. Even in modern institutions of higher education, the stellar attractions in the galaxy of scholarship often remain unavailable to students. They are names in college catalogues and prestigious journals, but few students receive the privilege of learning from them. Undergraduates in many large universities know all too well about the professor *in absentia*, whose courses graduate assistants handle. In a graduate program I encountered such a "phantom faculty" as an advisor. Each semester when I needed counsel, he was unavailable, "not in residence." Weary of waiting for him, I changed my program.

Jesus stayed often in the midst of His disciples. At His trial, Jesus reminded His accusers that He had made Himself available daily and taught the people openly (Luke 22:53). Nicodemus, himself an acknowledged teacher, was not denied an audience, even though he came at night (John 3:1, 2). At Sychar, Jesus was accessible at high noon (John 4:6). Anyone who desired to "learn of Him" needed but to come to Him (Matthew 11:28, 29). Only at the time of His destiny toward the cross did the Lord remove Himself from the public place. Jesus invited the people, "Come unto me," because He, the source of life and light, was always approachable.

Humble of Heart

Master-teachers possess a mind-set that realizes that self-abasement must precede advancement. The apostle Paul, who knew much about self-mastery, describes the process exemplified in the life of the Lord Jesus: "Let this mind be in you which was also in Christ Jesus" (Philippians 2:5). The Christ intelligence proves unlike the definitions assigned to intelligence today. With the increasing emphasis upon education for the "gifted" student, we have typically come to define intelligence in narrowly elitist terms. Superior intelligence unwisely connotes a smug and snobbish disdain for anyone with a merely average IQ. When one considers intelligence simply as the basis for admiration and accolades, it produces megalomaniacs, not masters. The Lord Jesus never saw a disparity between ability and humility. He who would become master must first become servant of all. The attitude of the master-teacher, as well as that of the model student, must include neither condescension nor contemptuousness. Jesus looked upon sinners as recipients of His saving grace, not as objects of scorn. Jesus, "filled with grace," always acted graciously. Greatness in any form does not exist apart from graciousness. Charles Garman, the master-teacher at Amherst College, said it so eloquently:

> The moral excellence, the personal loveliness of the pupil is the true crown of glory to a teacher. As well instruct a brute as a child, if the beauty of manhood or womanhood does not unfold, if no ambition, no aspiration after a noble life is awakened, if there are no bright dreams of the future. . . . To impress oneself

thus on an immortal being—an impression time can never efface—may well excite the envy of angels in Heaven.[15]

I recall the great teachers I've encountered as gracious people, too. They did not patronize or pander to me. They had too much regard for my dignity and their own integrity to fall into either perilous trap. Neither did they grasp for power or pretend infallibility. The paranoia that dominates power seekers and power holders never possessed our Lord. Confident in His capabilities, He exuded the quiet dignity of authority that was rightfully His and that He used only for the advantage of others.

The Voice of the Master

Authority is the credential of the master-teacher, and communication is his keynote. Although at times His reticence spoke more powerfully than speeches (Matthew 21:27; Matthew 27:14), Jesus never dodged responsible inquiry, and an honest question or request He always met with a straight and immediate reply. Christ was *the* great communicator; His was the voice of authority. The Word Incarnate said that which the Father had given Him to speak (John 12:50). Small wonder that some, astonished by His utterances, responded: "Never man spake like this man" (John 7:46).

The Master-Teacher is not a word waster. He does not speak simply to hear the sound of His own voice. The "wheat of the word" survives the winnowing that scatters the chaff of empty speech. Skeptics who use words to bewilder and confuse soon find their hollow sounds echoing in their own ears.

> *Mock on, Mock on Voltaire, Rousseau*
> *Mock on, Mock on: 'tis in vain!*
> *You throw the sand against the wind,*
> *and the wind blows it back again.*[16]

The Master-Teacher weighs His words and speaks of things eternal, and His words do not return void (Isaiah 55:11). His words are spirit and life (John 6:63), succinct yet eloquent, terse yet timeless. Without superfluity, they feed hungry hearts to the full. To His disciples these schoolboys of Galilee who will one day become teachers, He instructs in schoolyards beside the sea and on the summits.

The master-teachers always taught while seated. When Jesus evangelized, invariably, He stood and cried out. But His teaching was *ex cathedra,* "from the seat of authority." A stump or a boat or a well immediately became the scholar's chair—far superior, in its rustic setting, to any endowed chair in the most prestigious universities. His presence made the everyday august. What President Garfield said about the eminent teacher-scholar of Williams College, Mark Hopkins, can rightfully (and more meaningfully) be said of Christ: "Give me a log hut, with only a simple bench, Mark Hopkins at one end and I on the other, and you may have all the buildings, apparatus, and libraries without him."[17]

When the Master-Teacher spoke, He transformed the ordinary places into oracles.

A master-teacher must communicate masterfully. Lessons need to be articulated so the hearer finds them intelligible. The apostle Paul, an adept communicator, reminds us that all the verbiage in the world will accomplish nothing, if it is not understood. Better five words intelligibly spoken than a thousand words misunderstood (1 Corinthians 14:19). Jesus possessed verbal facility and a mastery of language. He was the elocutionist for the common man. He sought neither to impress His hearers nor to dazzle them with the pitchman's rhetoric. His words were poetically chosen and expressively spoken. With a graceful ease, He gathered the prosaic elements of life about Him and masterfully wove them into a rich fabric of living language. His voice, rich and resonant, could rival the silver-tongued orator's. His words, clean and uncluttered, communicated the mysteries of God in simple speech.

A teacher's greatest asset (or weapon?) is his capacity for communication. Vocal projection and verbal pellucidy combine to command attention from the least responsive audience. Recently my daughter commented on one of her university instructors. Although his physical presence was not particularly appealing, his voice, she said, mesmerized her. "I could listen to him all evening," she explained wistfully.

Oral communication skills (as well as facility in writing) contributed immensely to C. S. Lewis's popularity as an Oxford lecturer and Christian advocate. Lewis's biographer and former student admitted that Lewis "did not suddenly become the best lecturer . . . at Oxford: it was ten or fifteen years before such a description could be considered seriously."[18] Lewis lectured extensively and gave a series of talks about Christianity on the BBC. He was noted for his humor, command of his subject, and verbal facility. Identifying features that attracted audiences throughout the English-speaking world, a voice teacher who analyzed Lewis's vocal qualities declared: "Perhaps the most outstanding characteristic of Lewis' voice is the resonance. It has a richness of sound, an expansiveness and dimension, the sort of balanced tone you obtain by regulating the treble-bass dials on a stereophonic instrument. The resonance in combination with the baritone pitch gives an impression of masculinity and strength."[19] An examination of Lewis's radio recordings revealed an authoritative presence, a command of verbal space, and a rich range of language. In no small part his superior vocal quality enhanced. C. S. Lewis's appeal as a teacher and speaker.

> To me it sounds pleasant but not saccharine, confident but not cocksure, rich but not ponderous. . . . He speaks in a slow, evenly pitched voice and creates a drowsy, familiar or sorrowful mood. He ridicules by uttering words very slowly in a feigned solemnity and then rattling off others in rapid precision. He provides brief but choice moments of humor by giving imaginary dialogues in more than his usual pitch shifts. . . . all the while Lewis speaks with sense, fluency and exactness, his mind, eye and tongue working in flawless co-ordination.[20]

An infant settles down and ceases fretting at the reassuring sound of Mother's voice. Friendly voices give us confidence and security. Strident voices irritate and unnerve us. Voices full of energy call us to duty. Voices filled with empathy move us to tears.

Teachers know the value of the voice. We remember the great communicators by the sound of their voices. In an era without electronics and technology to move the voice vast distances, George Whitefield was renowned for his vocal projection and elocution. This eighteenth-century Oxford-educated preacher spoke to multitudes in open-air settings and captivated them by the magnificence of his speech. Benjamin Franklin, one of Whitefield's admirers, described what he heard: ". . . Every accent, every emphasis, every modulation of voice was so perfectly well turned and well placed, that without being interested in the subject, one could not help being pleased with the discourse; a pleasure of much the same kind with that received from an excellent piece of musick."[21]

The late British actor Richard Burton, who had a silvery and sublime voice, was interviewed on television several years ago. The show's host asked Burton to quote some fond passage from a favorite work, assuming Burton would quote from Shakespeare or one of his stage-show scripts. Instead Burton chose a most unlikely text. He told how books were often unavailable in the Welsh hills where he grew up, but the Bible was always available, and he had spent much time memorizing passages from it. Then with golden resonance, he recited from 2 Samuel 18. He began at verse 24 and electrified the audience with his cadence and vocal control, concluding with: "And the king was much moved, and went up to the chamber over the gate, and wept: and as he went, thus he said, O my son Absalom, my son, my son Absalom! would God I had died for thee, O Absalom, my son, my son!" The audience, which had listened in stunned silence to the flawless, tender interpretation, broke into vigorous and prolonged applause.

I imagine the voice of the Master—crystalline, with perhaps a hint of Galilean accent, to give it character. As He taught the multitudes on those occasions, without the aid of amplification, the mellifluous tones reverberated throughout the valleys and echoed from the hills. The hills of Galilee were alive with the sound of His music. What was said of A. W. Verrall, the Cambridge don, could be said of our Lord:

> He could read . . . so sonorously and melodiously that new meaning emerged from every line. He could lecture for an hour with closed eyes, leading his students in pursuit of a result which they might have rejected as nonsense if they had met it abruptly face to face, but which, after a long and exciting hunt, they seized with an eagerness largely created by the charm of their delightful guide.[22]

We dare not take the gift of human language for granted. Psycholinguist Noam Chomsky has convincingly demonstrated that language is innate in humans and no other species of animal life has anything comparable to it.[23] The great teachers have generally been men and women of voice. They may not have attained the eloquence of the Greek orator Demosthenes, but they have left impressions because of their controlled and convincing voices. In their utterances, we sense sincerity. They weave word spells that educate and enchant us. At times, their discourse involves nothing more than a series of monosyllables, but the patterns and arrangements imbue their words with a breathless beauty.

Jesus never took words for granted. He spoke with conviction, and His words were always inspired. From God He breathed in the words to speak, and He breathed them out, exhilaratingly, to ready ears and receptive hearts. In society today, which has cheapened speech and degraded verbal communication, we need to be alert to the exactness of the Master-Teacher's words. They were chosen with precision. Today, regrettably, we too casually and often crudely employ our words and typically reflect the attitude of Humpty Dumpty in Lewis Carroll's, *Through the Looking Glass:* "When I use a word, Humpty Dumpty said in a rather scornful tone, it means just what I choose it to mean—neither more nor less."[24]

Words are instruments intended for use in the most profound of human activities—communication—and Christ conceived of His speech as nothing less than the most serious of affairs concerning His Father's business. Lovers of language, like Edwin Newman, have underscored and lamented the woeful state of affairs into which the English language has fallen.[25] Eminent Christian apologist Robert Anderson was fond of saying that words were the coins of the wise and the counters of fools. If words do not mean what they are intended to mean, they become worse than useless.

Jesus, the Master-Teacher, had a rich repertoire of words that He used poetically and precisely. No stranger to the choice word or the poignant phrase, He drew His language from the lushness of the Palestinian landscape, fertile with ideas and imagery. Jesus never seems to have taught within the traditional environments of education. He had not acquired His own education through the conventional, highly formalized procedures. His critics charged Him with having had little traditional schooling: "How knoweth this man letters, having never learned?" (John 7:15). Yet He rightly deserved the title *Master-Teacher,* because as Nicodemus correctly asserted, He had come from God. Ultimately and unquestionably, the authoritative teaching comes from no other source. The Authorized Version of the Bible refers to our Lord's teaching as "doctrine." *Doctrine* refers to a body of teaching, just as the title *doctor* refers to a teacher of doctrine. The Jewish teachers of the Law engaged in teaching the vast body of interpretation that had grown up around the Law. Unlike their basis for instruction, the "Great Didactic" of Christ (to use Comenius's phrase)[26] came from God. Therefore, His teaching stood the unimpeachable test of divine integrity. Not mere opinion or shallow speculation or slavish tradition, it had, in J. B. Phillip's words, "the ring of truth." And truth will find its inevitable audience of intent listeners and learners who attend to the words of the Master-Teacher. When He speaks, His credentials are confirmed by the Voice from heaven: "This is my beloved Son, . . . hear ye him" (Matthew 17:5).

12
MASTER OF
THE METAPHOR

But without a parable spake he not unto them. . . .

Mark 4:34

Which things are an allegory. . . .

Galatians 4:24

> . . . and the writing
> be of words, slow and quick, sharp
> to strike, quiet to wait,
> sleepless
>
> through metaphor to reconcile
> the people and the stones. . . .[1]

One of the major difficulties with education today is that it is institutionalized. For the most part, formal education takes place in rigidly structured bureaucracies. Students must learn everything within walls, and to some extent, that injects an element of artificiality.

In a large, suburban high school in which I taught, students could not go outside the walls of the school building during the schoolday. Surrounding the school buildings were lushly landscaped grounds, with green grass soft and thick as a carpet. In pleasant weather, some teachers wanted to take their classes outdoors and let them listen to the lesson while lounging on the lawn. The administration would not permit it. A few unintimidated teachers crusaded for a bit more freedom for the students. These students, we reminded the administration, were almost adults (some *were* adults!). To restrict them to the buildings went contrary to good educational practice, we contended, not to mention good sense. That administrative edict sprang from the desire to *control*. Once outside the building, students presumably would become less manageable. We told the principal we'd take the chance; he finally relented. Chaos did not result.

Pictures of the Unknown

When the Lord Jesus taught, He made the outdoors His auditorium. Unless we are aware of the Oriental approach to learning, we find it difficult to understand the methods and figures of speech in His instruction. In the Eastern world, the art of oral instruction was common, and itinerant teachers abounded. They would walk about and travel to find pupils. Ancient Athens knew of its "peripatetic philosophers," who gave lectures while "on the walk."

Quite naturally Jesus chose His examples from the landscape about Him. The cornucopia of commonplace experiences supplied Him with examples and metaphors. His sensitivity to every situation enriched His visual and verbal repertoire. I had a Sunday-school teacher like that, who possessed a quick wit and a ready illustration for everything. "Having the Bible available is like having a pair of shoes," he would say. "Reading the Bible is like putting the shoes on your feet. Applying what you read is like tying the shoelaces. Everything is snug, comfortable, and you walk so much better in life."

Jesus was a master of the metaphor. G. Campbell Morgan claims the Sermon on the Mount contains forty-nine metaphors.[2] According to the poet John Ciardi, "all metaphor is basically a way of speaking of the unknown in terms of the known."[3] The teacher has the task of leading the student from the known to the unknown, from the obvious to the obscure. Wise teachers couch their lessons in phrases and figures familiar to the learners. Obfuscation should never be the teacher's intention. Our Lord never used parables to becloud issues, but rather, as Morgan explained, to employ an approach especially suited to clarify.

A cursory examination of the plethora of parables Jesus used alerts us immediately to the progression of truth He unfolded. Beginning His teaching with simple statements, illustrated by commonplace incidents, He then moved toward more complex mysteries. The seminal parable the Lord presented to the multitudes who met Him along the beach served as the seed from which all parables would grow. The parable of the Sower was fundamental, Christ asserted, for understanding all others (Mark 4:13). Jesus took the quite familiar chore of sowing or broadcasting seeds to teach how life develops in the believer and how the kingdom of God develops. Any traveler to Palestine today would immediately see how sensible the illustration was. The different soils represented different types of reception the seed received. The adamant, path hardened, would repel any seed. The surface soil hid the rock below it and would provide no depth for any other than a short-lived shoot or two. The potentially fertile soil, overgrown with thickets, was not conducive to fruitfulness. But the good soil, free from thorns and cultivated to enhance life, allows the crops to flourish. The parable paralleled the spiritual life that was the ultimate goal of our Lord's teaching. His objective was not to give a lesson in agriculture or farming. This parabolic (Greek: *parabole* "thrown alongside") story would set the scene for the greater truth in the realm of spiritual realities. During an extended period of His teaching ministry, our Lord said nothing without the aid of parables (Matthew 13:34). He found His hearers so dull (as Isaiah had predicted, Isaiah 6:9; Matthew 13:13, 14), that He had to resort to storytelling to penetrate the crust of their incomprehension. Parables were earthly stories with a heavenly truth.

In classical literature, one famous parable used for similar purposes was Plato's "Parable of the Cave." In it, a group of people chained to a wall watched shadows projected upon it by a fire in the background. Unable to see beyond, the cave dwellers mistakenly assumed the shadowy representations were reality. In the parable, one cave dweller frees himself from the shackles and makes his way toward a lighted opening in the rear of the cave and manages to escape into the sunlight of the real world and then hastens to liberate the others.[5] The point of the parable is this: Mankind is locked in a cave of sensory impressions, which deal only with a shadowy world of imperfection. Beyond that world of the senses exists a world of spirit, and to know that world is to know God and truth.

Patiently and systematically, in picture form, the Master-Teacher unfolds startlingly transcendent truths. Jesus knew that man was a "metaphoric animal" and the "natural man" (1 Corinthians 2:14) needed natural representations. Christ would scan the sky and bring the bird into the disciples' field of vision. God cares for sparrows, which could be bought for next to nothing. Plentiful and cheap, the sparrows symbolized a valueless commodity. Jesus drove home the lesson of God's loving care. The sparrow, flitting back and forth, going from place to place, finds a nesting place on God's altar. Will not the heavenly Father provide rest for His own children? The raven sits in the tree, big and black—the scavenger of the roadways. A vulture's appetite. Insatiable! Your Father in heaven feeds that bird. Will He not feed you?

What charming choices Jesus makes to get the point across! Fluffy balls of white dot the mountainside. Shepherds—the ubiquitous figures, who spend lonely days leading their flocks to pastures, guarding them from predators, and returning them to the fold at evening. "I am the Good Shepherd," Jesus announces. Immediately, the imagery emerges in their minds. *You are My sheep—helpless, dependent, incapable of your own protection—unequipped to deal with the constant dangers that threaten your welfare. Do not fear. True shepherds guard their flocks.* The intimacy established between sheep and shepherd inspired songs of ancient legend and lore and celebrated the loyalty in that relationship. That's the way it is between the Master and us.

I once taught sixth-grade students, boys and girls at that curious, eager age, when the world seemed alive with learning and they needed few goads to learning. Our classroom was situated in the angle of two buildings, which formed an L. The lesson that period was fairly routine, and everyone was actively involved. Suddenly, a voice broke through the serious mutterings: "Look, that cat's after those squirrels." Outside the window, two squirrels, oblivious to the cat's presence, frisked in the autumn foliage. They scampered about in the leaves, picked up acorns, and chased each other playfully. The cat started at the extreme end of the building and silently, stealthily, stalked the squirrels. The class ran to the windows. "Quietly," I cautioned them. They huddled around the glass and had front-row seats. The cat, step by step, with infinite patience, crept along, stopping whenever it suspected it had been spotted.

"Do you think the cat has a chance?" I asked.

"Nah. Those squirrels are too quick. He'll never get them," one boy answered confidently.

"All they have to do is run up a tree if he comes," a girl suggested.

"They'll get wind of his scent before he gets too close,"

another student offered. "No way that cat will ever get that close."

The muted conversation continued the entire time the cat stalked its prey. It took more than ten minutes before it made its move and darted after the squirrels. One squirrel ran quickly up a tree, but the other squirrel fell victim to its predator.

"Tell me what you saw." I asked the class. "What lessons did you learn?"

We continued for the rest of the class period, examining the cat's strategy and the squirrels' recklessness, the cat's patience and the squirrels' peril. The students applied the lessons to their own lives. The cat and the squirrels became a parable for the class, and we used the real-life lesson in nature to learn about human life.

Prepared to Teach

The Lord Jesus did not simply and unthinkingly grasp whatever was available. Instead He did everything strategically and purposefully. Christ attended to His surroundings and selected wisely, because He was thoroughly familiar with His subject. He had saturated Himself with the topic He taught and consequently, recognized the relationships in the environment about Him. John Dewey has identified several prerequisites for good teachers. The first and fundamental requirement is: know your subject thoroughly—have it "at finger tips' end" in Dewey's words. I have watched teachers perform who claimed to rely solely upon spontaneity. Some have even boasted that they went into the classroom without a predetermined topic or preconceived pattern. Usually their classes were dull, often chaotic, and they fostered student indifference. I suspect laziness rather than spontaneity motivated the unprepared teachers.

Preparation is imperative for effective pedagogy. Ignorance begets ignorance. We simply can find no substitute for knowledge. Of course knowledge by itself is not the only goal of education, but what you don't know *can* hurt you. Depth of knowledge has great benefits. One cannot swim in the water of superficiality. Unfortunately in some quarters, Christians recite the sentimental slogan "a little knowledge is a dangerous thing," to discredit education. Like Festus's reaction to Paul, some people believe "much learning doth make thee mad" (Acts 26:24). A little knowledge is, indeed, dangerous. Students of the Master-Teacher must immerse themselves.

> A little learning is a dangerous thing;
> Drink deep, or taste not the Pierian
>   spring:
> There shallow draughts intoxicate the brains
> and drinking largely sobers us again.[6]

Teachers and students need to saturate themselves in vital subjects; Christian stewardship demands it. Like ignorance of the law, ignorance of truth and knowledge is no excuse and is inexcusable. The eternal truths and ultimate realities with which the Savior dealt were not vagaries but verities. When I sit in the presence of someone who knows what he's talking about, I always feel impressed. I can tolerate ineffective presentations; I can abide the monotonous drone of an unreflective voice; I can bear with the all-too-frequent *uhs* and distracting idiosyncrasies. But I cannot condone ignorance that parades as knowledge.

Prepared to Learn

All believers in Christ should be perpetual pupils. We should give ourselves ceaselessly to knowing as much as we can about whatever endeavor we pursue. Add knowledge and add *to* knowledge, Peter advises (2 Peter 1:5, 6). Hosea lamented that God's people were destroyed for a lack of knowledge (Hosea 4:6). A four-step model has been identified for the creative process. Presumably, new discoveries and original insights occur according to this pattern—and the first step is *preparation*. Incubation, illumination, and verification follow. Creative genius knows that preparation and perspiration come prior to inspiration.

Often I encounter students, eager to get going in their professional lives, who see their educational years as an unwarranted intrusion. Some profess the need for no further study. "I'm ready to get out there and do my job," they state confidently. Students who aspire to vocations peculiarly Christian in their calling sometimes feel fettered with all the preparation. "All I need is the Lord, and I can move mountains," they say with that far-off look of ecstasy in their eyes. I remind them that when God moves mountains Himself, it's done by means of earthquakes, but when He needs to tunnel through to make roads, He usually calls for engineers. When God calls people to His work, it is always specifically "for the work whereunto I have called them" (Acts 13:2), and that specific work imposes restrictions and qualifications. There is a human reality that God will not violate. When William Carey, the father of the modern missionary movement, felt led of God to go to India, he undertook intensive instruction in a number of languages and eventually became so proficient, he received an academic title in recognition of that accomplishment.

Nineteenth-century amateur archaeologist Heinrich Schliemann set out to excavate the ancient cities of Troy and Mycenae, armed with his dog-earred copy of Homer's *Iliad*. Heroic epics of ancient wars fired his imagination but before he undertook the task of unearthing cities whose discovery startled the world, he schooled himself in classical Greek and a dozen other languages. Our Lord Jesus knew God's word so well that He could use it with incomparable effectiveness to guide Him not to the bowels of the earth but to the depths of man's being.

A Vital Message

Although Jesus used the imagery of people's lives, He never dwelt indulgently or excessively in the prosaic pictures of life. Even the most vivid imagery eventually dulls the vision when it is repeated too much. The monotonous refrain soon loses its charm. The most awe-inspiring landscape becomes just another pretty picture when you live among it every day. Fresh images, tactfully chosen, enliven lessons that allow for their easy recall and application. Creative teachers continually cull new expressions that provide them with fresh ways of saying old things. Old things need not become stale things if they are refreshed frequently and seasoned with the vitality and charm of a new saying.

> The teacher who would find his way to the hearts and understandings of his hearers, will never keep down the parabolic element of his teaching, but will make as frequent use of it as he can. To do this effectually, will need a fresh effort of his own; for while all language is more or less figurative, yet long use has worn out the freshness of the stamp, so that, to create a powerful impression, language must be cast into novel forms, as was done by our Savior.[7]

Using nature, Jesus stirred up images in the mind. Quite possibly, God fashioned creation for this specific purpose: to elicit a response within mankind. To sensitive hearts, the natural world is a wondrous parable figuratively reflecting bits and fragments of God's power, purpose, and paternal care. The Word of God, in its declaration about God, corresponds with the works in their demonstration of God: "Now the whole of Scripture, with its constant use of figurative language, is a re-awakening of man to the mystery of nature, and giving back to him the key of knowledge: and this comes out in its highest form . . . in the parables."[8]

A Vital Purpose

But our Lord's way with words and His metaphoric wit were not for the pleasure that His voice gave to words. He did not solely choose His phrases for "purely percussive purposes" (to borrow Archibald MacLeish's expression). Form and function wed together in verbal harmony, and the marriage of His message with metaphor and parable impressed the lesson with laser permanency in the hearts of His hearers.

The apostle John, more than the other disciples, possessed a poetic appreciation of the expressive quality of Christ, for he records the allusions the Lord made to Himself and the timely metaphors by which He conveyed His power and provision: "I am the light of the world!" "I am the way, the truth, and the life!" "I am the door!" "I am the good shepherd!" "I am the bread of life!" "I am the true vine!" "I am the resurrection and the life!" Each one communicated the lesson Jesus taught. If Christ had declared, propositionally, that He could provide nourishment and sustain His people in all difficulties, they might not have fully comprehended. But none can mistake the intention in "I am the bread of life." In a world where bread was the staff of life, the staple of the diet, the message came across unmistakably. If Jesus had decided to give a learned discourse on the Holy Spirit and the gifts He bestows, his auditors might have misunderstood, but saying "Out of his innermost being shall flow rivers of living water" (see John 7:38), would perk up the ears of the crowd. Life-giving water, reminiscent of the flow from the rocks at Horeb and Kadesh, aptly described it. The people would nod knowingly. If their water supply were cut off, they would perish. Thirst was a haunting specter over a land that faced the constant peril of drought. John wrote down what the Master said, and those images continue to impress themselves on our minds. They are universal in meaning and application, and although culture and climate may change, the meaning behind the metaphor remains.

The noble aims and lofty intentions of some teachers are thwarted because of the stunted growth of their verbal imagery. Pedantic and trite exposition needs the enrichment and invigoration of life's daily expressions. Modes of teaching must tap into the limitless symbolism in the natural world.[9]

Literal mindedness has its limitations. If we traffic as verbal vendors where a word has one, fixed meaning, we will need a lot of literary coinage to buy and sell ideas. The grandeur of the metaphor frees us from these simple and simplistic approaches to learning. God Himself created rapturously rich languages. In His own word to us, He delights to engage our thinking with ever exquisitely enriching images of Himself and His creation. "The love of logical tidiness," as Kidner put it, treats language too much like a procrustean bed.[10] We too eagerly chop off, compress, and in the process, destroy the message that comes to us. What too often some perjoratively term "flowery phraseology" is the only kind of language that attracts the labor of the bees and that produces any honey (not to mention fragrance). Jesus would not be too welcome, I suppose, in the many modern institutions where "literalist" language is *de rigueur*.

I spoke to an audience using a text from Matthew's Gospel. In my attempts to communicate the imagery of Christ as the majestic King, I said: "The King strides regally across the pages of this Gospel, holding out His invisible scepter of sovereignty and dispelling all opposition to His claim." After the meeting, a woman told me how much she liked the phrases and how it had captivated her (she probably forgot everything else I said). I felt like clapping my hands for joy, and rephrasing Browning's line: "A man's speech should exceed his gasp, or what's a metaphor?"

13

THE MASTER LESSON

A wise man will hear, and will increase learning; and a man of understanding shall attain unto wise counsels.

Proverbs 1:5

Did you learn your lesson?
Did you know it well?
Do you learn your lesson?
Only time will tell.

ANONYMOUS

The student of Scripture is constantly impressed by its amazing and unfailing candor. It never condones a single human fault or palliates a single human weakness. . . . One of the first lessons . . . taught was this: it was the insufficiency of cleverness.[1]

In a summer session seminar I once attended, the director presented what he called "the master lesson." He told the students that the lesson was the quintessential presentation for that topic; it had been developed in accordance with all that we know a lesson should be. It conformed in content, style, development, presentation, delivery, and impact upon hearers to the most rigorously researched criteria yet developed for a learning experience. Because of its perfection of conception, content, and consequences, we call it a master lesson. "I am not a master-teacher," he hastened to add, "but what I am about to present to you is, incontrovertibly, a master lesson."

The Master's Lesson

Beneath the cloudless Galilean sky, our Lord ascends the Mount, with His select group of disciples huddled about Him. The Teacher sets Himself for the Grand Proclamation—*the* lecture—*the* master lesson. The lesson, primarily ethical in character, he directs toward developing the character of His disciples, for Jesus knows that content divorced from character ultimately damages. Upon the Mount of Beatitudes the Master-Teacher declares the elements of His educational community. His words atop this knoll are as much a lecture as a sermon. Because He will discourse about heaven-sent things, He must temporarily remove His disciples from the cacophony of the busy world at the mountain's base. Foreign as they may sound, the lessons these men will need to learn Law will become the basis for transforming the society in which they move. Geoffrey Bull senses the significance of this locution: ". . . At the summit Jesus speaks alone. There is no discussion, no voicing of opinion, no alternative suggestion. . . . The Christ is set upon the hill and we can only come to Him and listen to the Word He speaks, a Word so final and so complete that when heaven and earth dissolve it still shall stand. Such then is our Master. No wonder that His word so quickly shakes our puny thoughts to pieces."[2]

The scene is hushed and holy as the Master-Teacher unlocks the secret to the spiritual life for the students and reveals, through paradox, the principles of His own pedagogy. God reserves blessing for the "poor in spirit" as well as the "meek" and "pure in heart." Jesus talks first about the inner qualities, because He knows that commendation begins in the inner life. Mastery must first take place in the heart and soul—in one's own citadel. Before we can take other territory, we must master the sphere of the spiritual. Only "disciples indeed" (John 8:31) surround Him at the summit. There they will hear "hard sayings" (John 6:60), which the dilettante will find distasteful. The multitudes have peeled away as Christ has moved upward. Elevations deter all but the truly devoted, who seek the rarefied atmosphere of truth; devoted disciples alone willingly defy the gravity that drives the less committed back to ground level. Only after the Master-Lesson has been taught on the mountaintop can the students return to sea level: ". . . He went up into a mountain: and when he was set, his disciples came unto him: And he opened his mouth and taught them. . ." (Matthew 5:1, 2).

Disciples are students. The Greek work *mathetes* (from which we get our English word *mathematics*), translated "disciple," identifies a learner—someone taught by a teacher. That role involves serious thinking and obedient action; the learner listens attentively to the words of the master and then acts affirmatively upon them. Though multitudes may meander at the base of the mountain, they do not climb with any seriousness. Their direction is much too lateral; their interests are too easily distracted by side noises. Only true learners climb *this* day.

F. B. Meyer colorfully captures the setting of the windless day when light and love were revealed on a hilltop:

. . . He ascends by a long and easy slope of unfenced common land, the grace of which was embroidered with daisies, white and red anemones, blue hyacinths, and the yellow-flowered clover. . . . After a gradual ascent of three or four miles, he reached at length a crater-like space with a slightly hollow floor set in a frame of rough crags, and strewn with boulders and fragments of black asphalt—. Above, the hill rose up into two high grassy knolls, some sixty feet in height, known as the Horns of Hattin. . . . He might have selected for his oratory the summit of one of those grassy knolls. . . . On the southwest the huge cone of Tabor; to the north the majestic lake; far away on its other side the precipitous cliffs of Gadara rising sheer from its shore; no signs of human habitation; no sound of earthly toil; no fear of intrusion . . . —such was the oratory, whose soft grass was trodden by those blessed feet. . . .[3]

Jesus employed the gnomic (Greek: "wise saying") technique in teaching His disciples, which "begins abruptly with a single mystical assertion for which an equally mystical reason is given."[4] He does not ramble on incoherently as teachers who try to "cover material" often do. He stops strategically (the pregnant pause) to let his listeners assimilate the words. The rhythm of His voice (meter is heavily the Hebraic preference), with its rise and fall, its accent and emphasis, its subtle nuances, deepens the impression. The words, rendered slowly and meditatively, deliberate and mnemonically constructed, comprise the discourse. This is the test of true teaching—does the student relate to and remember what he hears? How many recall the last lecture? In part, the problem stems from inattentive and undisciplined hearers. But teachers, unconcerned about the preciseness of their speech or the lyrical quality of their voices, lull students into indifference. A word, judiciously and tastefully chosen, can never, in fact, substitute for another. There is no such thing as a synonym! The more varied and vibrant the teacher's vocabulary, the more melodic and memorable the message. Only a true Paganini can play a symphonic work on *one* violin string!

O the Blessedness!

The Master-Teacher begins with statements of blessedness. In quick succession, staccatolike, He announces the Godlike character of disciples who seek to cultivate virtues society arrogantly dismisses as worthless. *Blessedness* (Greek: *makarios*) is too timidly translated by the word "happy." *Makarios* conjures up images of sublime and serene realities that transcend the "life adjustment" approach to education. Jesus does not enjoin His listeners to accommodate to culture. He teaches transformation! He reverses prevailing customs with simple but potent homilies.

Who today would base a curriculum upon renunciation? Quaint characters like Gandhi, viewed from a distance as objects of amused admiration, have attracted adherents in their day. But today's technological culture values movement and mobility up the hierarchy of organizational life; it sees education as the means to enhance that movement. Commonly, people view schools as places "to get ahead." Students go there to get better jobs and more status, which give them access to all the creature comforts, a technological and satiated society calls success. That's why these claims of Christ are revolutionary today. They cut diametrically across the grain of "get ahead-ism." They challenge the notions that imprison people in their cells of self-preoccupation.

The ejaculatory beginning, "O the blessedness. . . ," promises liberation to students who desire to learn the difficult and unpopular lessons. With the melody of the mountains, Jesus frees spirits to soar and burst the fetters of material bondage. At gray dawn in Auschwitz prison, Victor Frankl experienced something akin to that emancipation. Above the prison camp, the sun vainly searched for an opening in a thick layer of clouds. At best, its light cast a somber radiance over the dreary place. Awakened to the dull drudgery of another hopeless day, Frankl carried on his secret conversation with his absent wife. He could survive, he thought, if only he could find a reason for his suffering. Deprived of the tenderness of companionship, void of any prospects for release, and disillusioned by life's sad lot, he sought to make sense of a senseless world. But like music that serenaded the Mount on the day of the Master's talk, Frankl was transported within touch of heaven.

> In a last violent protest against hopelessness of im-
> minent death, I sensed my spirit piercing through the
> enveloping gloom. I felt it transcend that hopeless,
> meaningless world and from somewhere I heard a vic-
> torious "Yes" in answer to my question of the exis-
> tence of an ultimate purpose. At that moment a light
> was lit . . . and the light shineth in darkness. . . .
> Then, at that very moment, a bird flew down silently
> and perched in front of me. . . .[5]

As Jesus speaks, a light appears in darkness. "Blessed are. . . ." Birds from the heavens settle on that holy hill. The master lesson brings blessing. With a rich resonance, the Beatitudes ring and reverberate among those hills, and we still hear their echo in every classroom where blessings flow. Blessing came to Helen Keller, a child without sight or hearing, the day her teacher, the miracle worker, entered her life: "I felt approaching footsteps. I stretched out my hand. . . . Someone took it, and I was caught up and held close in the arms of her who had come to reveal all things to me, and more than all things, to love me."[6]

As teachers enrich their students' lives, taking them beyond the veil of time and sense, they shine light in dark places. Teachers should start every class period with the ecstatic benediction of the Beatitudes: *Makarios!* "Blessed are ye!" In Greek-speaking cultures, Christians greet Easter morning with the joyous proclamation *Christos anesti,* "Christ is risen!" And the reply always comes, *Anesti alethia*—"He is risen indeed!" Each new schoolday provides an opportunity for resurrection in the classroom. The resurrection of young minds eager to learn is far more revolutionary than any military conquest. Teachers who have targeted their approach to bring about intellectual and spiritual revolutions know the potential for their plans.

In their eight-fold unfolding of blessedness, the Beatitudes conform to what Geoffrey Bull has called "the central octave of the whole range of heavenly truth." Their musical movement builds up to a crescendo. "With the touch of the Master's hand" the notes, each successively pitched higher than the last, form the lesson in character development. "From these eight notes all moral harmony is formed."[7] Jesus says, "blessed are the poor in spirit: for theirs is the kingdom of heaven." The first note, with vibratolike force, strikes the key, and blessedness rings and resonates in the soul. In ordered sequence, the Master leads His listeners up the moral octave. Each pronouncement, followed by a reflective pause, moves the student to the next level. Progressively, the "they shalls" follow the "blessed ares" linking qualities and consequences, unfolding like a flower petal; and soon beauty and brilliance emerge in exquisite symmetry. This type of teaching is not soon forgotten. The sensation experienced by the Master-Teacher that day was not unlike Gilbert Highet's peak experience as a teacher: "For one of the greatest pleasures in teaching comes from those hours when you feel that every word you say is being heard, not by a collection of bored and dutiful individuals, but instead by a group which you create and which in turn creates you; that instead of repeating facts learnt by rote, to be telephoned through the drowsy air to half-dead ears and garbled down in notebooks, you are . . . stirring minds. . . ."[8]

Reinforcing the Metaphors

At the conclusion of the Beatitudes, the Master-Teacher selects the appropriate similes to illustrate and reinforce the teaching. The strategic placement of word pictures does much to vivify a lesson. Taking common examples from everyday life, Jesus illustrated the blessed life. He chooses salt and light. In a world where spoilage and corruption were commonplace, salt readily symbolized preservation, a deterrent to decay. If the qualities of blessedness operate within, then that life will impede spoilage and enhance taste. Your *blessed* life will penetrate the mass of humanity and will season it with spiritual salt. When the inner life of the spirit pulsates with the heartbeat of God, the moral virtue will manifest itself in practical and public ways. "Salt is the Christian in his moral character permeating the mass through personal contact. . . . Salt brings out the true flavor of things thus defining the nature of that with which it comes in contact."[9] In that day, life could not survive without salt. It symbolized the private, blessed life as it penetrated society, checking the ignoble growth of evil, flavoring relationships, and adding savor to society.

From the mountain on which Jesus taught, the disciples have an unobstructed view of the surrounding countryside and the small towns that dot the landscape. One city within view is suspended on a hillside, and as those eager eyes look off in the direction toward which the Master motions, that city stands in bold relief. "Ye are the light of the world. A city that is set on an hill cannot be hid" (Matthew 5:14). Light does its work by illumination. It shows things for what they are. The blessed life will reveal the flaws of a feckless world. "Like that city," Jesus was saying, "objects will be brought into clearer focus by your life. Shadows that obscure reality will disappear when the light of truth illumines life."

"Shine for Me in a dark world" is the Master's plea. "Brighten the dismal places and bring glory to God." "Light is the Christian in his moral character illuminating society by its public impact. . . . Light reveals the true color of things thus defining that upon which it makes its impact."[10]

What apt expressions Jesus uses! Master-teachers unlock hidden treasures with the key of expression. A picture cannot substitute for words, but pictures enhance words, and word-pictures combine the beauty and benefit of both. One of the greatest tools a teacher has is the simple phrase: "In other words. . . ." Elaboration and embellishment drive the lesson home and give it more ready reception in the learner. In reference to the eighth chapter of Romans, a teacher once said, "Paul climbed the alpine heights of rhetoric and reached the Matterhorn of God's magnificent declaration of justification in Christ.'' That priceless phrase has ever since been locked for safekeeping within my imaginary verbal vault where I store other equally precious phrases. I ponder them often and occasionally, parade them about as my own (plagiaristically). Unlike the written word, the spoken word becomes the common property of all who will own it. Much of our Lord's phraseology imbued itself within the disciples, and their writings owe their richness to His influence.

The master lesson ends. It took much of the day to deliver it. The lecture was not delivered from dog-eared notes, but from the freshness of the Master's own mandate. His startling words contrast with the stale impoverishment of the expressions ''of old time'' (Matthew 5:21), parroted banalities that constituted the course of study of the scribes. Refreshingly new, Jesus' syllabus lived with the energy of a redefinition of God's design for the blessed life. To paraphrase the Psalmist: ''a day in the school of the Master-Teacher is better than a thousand with the petty pedagogues.'' As He transforms a familiar setting into a lyceum the lecture rings in their ears, takes root in their hearts, and the vivid imagery dances before their spiritual eyes. What was the reaction to this teaching? Elton Trueblood of Earlham College tells of the lecture, entitled ''Acropolis and Aereopagus,'' which he gave on the ancient Acropolis in Athens. He concluded by saying: ''As a teacher of philosophy, it has been my dream for forty-five years that I might some day pay my respects to both kinds of nobility by lecturing to students in Athens. I have now done so.''[11]

Trueblood remarks that at the conclusion of his lecture, ''the 150 mature American students engaged in applause.'' Applause did not greet the end of Christ's lesson. After the master lesson concluded, ''. . . the people were astonished at his doctrine'' (Matthew 7:28). With mouths agape and eyes wide open, they greeted the teaching with jubilant incredulity. Finally, they had found One who spoke and taught with ability and authority (Matthew 7:29).

Part IV
THE FINAL EVALUATION

What is the chief goal of education? How do we determine or know what a student has really learned? With Pilate we ask, "What is truth?" Let's look at the end results of education, in all realms of life: material and spiritual.

14

GOD'S TRUTH IS ALL TRUTH

Study to shew thyself approved unto God. . . .

2 Timothy 2:15

Youth should be aw'd, possess'd, as with a sense
religious, of what holy joy there is
in knowledge, if it be sincerely sought
for its own sake, in glory, and in praise,
if but by labour won, and to endure.[1]

Teachers have hotly debated the goals of education for years, with each new generation proposing its particular interpretation and prescribing its own program. Philosophically, the debate spans the spectrum from pragmatism to perennialism. Pragmatist John Dewey identified *change* as the fundamental feature of human existence. Society continuously evolves and assumes new forms and styles, he declared. Those of his school of thought define human intelligence as the capacity for interaction with the environment. "Using problem-solving strategies, each generation shapes society according to its new knowledge and needs," they exclaim. "Nothing ever stays the same, and in the world of values and knowledge, we accept the creed of *relativism.* Experience alone links successive generations, and experience is always in a state of flux. Therefore we define education as the 'reconstruction of experience.' " Dewey explains: "We thus reach a technical definition of education: It is that reconstruction or reorganization of experience which adds to the meaning of experience, and which increases ability to direct the course of subsequent experience. . . . An activity which brings education or instruction with it makes one aware of some of the connections which had been imperceptible."[2]

To the pragmatists, education should guide change so that growth occurs. Few perceive random change or activity as desirable; they believe human intelligence provides for the conscious, systematic ordering of purposeful change to deal with new demands and new environments. Nothing is final or ultimate in a philosophical sense.

On the other hand, perennialism contends that there exists "eternal verities" that never change and have their origins in the mind of God. For perennialists, intelligence means, to use Newton's words, "O God, I think thy thoughts after thee!"[3] Robert Hutchins, former chancellor of the University of Chicago and foremost thinker among the perennialists, identifies the intellectual part of man (*Homo sapiens:* "man, the wise") as the essentially human in the higher order of life. Things of "time and sense" are less real than things of mind and spirit. Truth is unchanging and unchangeable. Education involves the teaching of truth; since truth never changes, education always remains the same. Herman Horne's definition of education would parallel that of Hutchins: "Education is the eternal process of superior adjustment of the physically and mentally developed, free, conscious human being to God, as manifested in the intellectual, emotional, and volitional environment of man."[4]

Education's Goals

Goals in education involve the philosophical realm of *teleology,* "end results," but God's purposes for mankind are not locked in time. Dewey's naturalistic explanations of human nature and the educational programs based on them do not prove adequate for the Christian, who derives his direction from the Bible. As the pinnacle of His creation, God endowed man with capacities and capabilities that transcend the natural sphere of existence. Admittedly, education must involve the world of sense, but it dare not limit itself to that. Christian education encompasses the broad eternal purposes of God and involves the critical spiritual dimension of man. "Man's chief end [goal]," states the Westminster Catechism, is to "glorify God and enjoy him for ever." Man remains incomplete without God, and education *must* address this vital relationship. Augustine thought intently about the role of learning and concluded, "Learning must begin with an exploration of the self; it culminates in an understanding of the nature of God."[5] The ultimate goal of all education must deal with "the eternal reasons of things."

Education should develop a person into the fullness of God-intended humanity. To be "human" in the most noble sense is to manifest the virtues displayed in Christ Jesus. In cultivating qualities that allow us to "come in the unity of the faith, and of the knowledge of the Son of God, unto a perfect man, unto the measure of the stature of the fulness of Christ" (Ephesians 4:13), education nears its goal.

The very human life we *now* live forms the context of our education; all learning takes place in a "cultural context." Because we *are* people of culture, we cannot live or grow without being educated by it. Tension between culture (in which we live) and critique of culture (to which God calls us as believers) contribute to the ambivalence some Christians have had toward education. Is the learning of the "world" to be shunned? Has schooling in the classical "liberal arts" simply accommodated secularism? Has the world forced us to swallow a pagan pill?

Saint Augustine, who unquestionably loved God fiercely, strongly advocated study of the liberal arts: "The souls of those who have not drunk from the fountain of the liberal arts are, as it were, hungry and famished; this is a condition of sterility."[6] The curriculum of the medieval cathedral schools included the seven liberal arts, and the Cathedral of Chartres in France, built principally in the twelfth century, merged the Gothic architecture of the church with the representations of the seven liberal arts of classical learning. Even the Virgin Mary was presumed to possess the seven liberal arts, and Thomas Aquinas affirmed her perfect knowledge of them. Such an association strains the relationship between the sacred life and secular learning a bit; nevertheless, we begin to see a link between the increasingly significant role of learning and the lives of the devoted.

More recently, Arthur Holmes, Wheaton College philosopher, embraced "liberal learning" as "an open invitation to join the human race and become more fully human."[7] The liberal arts of classical learning constitute, he contends, the best that is human, and participating in this learning involves becoming more fully human. "Liberal education is an opportunity to become more fully a human person in the image of God, to see life whole rather than fragmented, to transcend the provincialism of our place in history, our geographical location or our job. . . . It is an opportunity to find meaning for everything I am and do."[8]

Not every Christian subscribes to this exalted notion of liberal education. Some may find it dangerous and an invitation to flirt with the seductions of paganism (or at least to become secular). The affinity for classical thought has become associated with worldly philosophies of nature "less hostile to the things of this world than traditional Christian doctrine."[9] Many have accused conservative Christianity of "anti-intellectualism" at points in its development and of breeding a narrow religious provincialism. The tension between a Christian "spiritual" orientation and classical learning's "natural perspective" has scared off many believers.

What Is Truth?

For some, so-called "secular education" has been in part sanctified by the rubric "All truth is God's truth." Presumably, according to this slogan, God manifests truth in a general revelation, and approaches to investigation and inquiry (such as reason and science) are legitimate and acceptable. The creation mandate (Genesis 1:28) is the rationale for secular study: "The biblical concept of creation imparts sanctity to all realms of nature and to history and culture of man. This is my Father's world. . . . We therefore approach the works of God, probe their mysteries, and harness their potentialities with humility but with boldness as well. . . . To neglect the kind of education that helps us understand and appreciate God's world betrays either shallow thinking or fearful disbelief."[10]

An uncritical acceptance of all spheres of study as within the cultural or creation mandate appears risky to me. I experience a hesitancy (fearful disbelief?) to start at any point except God: *God's truth* is all truth! Human nature lost its creation innocence, and a diabolical power, assuming deceptive guises, counterfeits the claims of God in creation. Paul was not timid in declaring to the educated Greeks of his day that "the world by wisdom knew not God" and that "the natural man receiveth not the things of the Spirit of God: for they are foolishness unto him . . .'' (1 Corinthians 1:21, 2:14). Yet clearly Paul had received education in both Hebraic and Hellenic studies.

Faith and Learning

The great Christian minds have evidenced a compatibility of faith and learning. F. B. Meyer's devotional writings are replete with references to both classical writers and his own English poets and philosophers. George Morrison feels at home with British poetry and cites it routinely in his writings. Jonathan Edwards, noted for his uncompromising biblical proclamations, which fanned the flames of revival in eighteenth century New England, belonged to the Royal Scientific Society of Britain. And C. S. Lewis has forever dispelled the notion that learning and the Christian faith are not compatible. The enviable record of scholarship, writing, music, and poetry produced by men of vigorous Christian faith attests to the affinity of faith and knowledge. As Augustine noted: Faith seeks understanding.

Of course, we must not gullibly adopt current fashion, but instead constantly subject our experiences to the canon of God's Word. We must think ''Christianly'' about the issues and agendas of the times. In order to know and move about in our world, we must become informed and educated. But we are not simply bystanders (although we are pilgrims) who participate in society when it feels convenient and exploit its resources for certain ''spiritual goals.'' Although the value system of the social order lies under the control of the ''god of this world,'' the earth belongs to the Lord. Intellect, creativity, passion, and physical activity are elements in human life, and each, in relationship with all others, has a legitimate function. Language and logic (the critical core of the seven liberal arts) enhance worship, devotion, and godly submission. Faith finds its fullest expression, not in ignorance, but in enlightened awareness of God's gifts and in sanctified human potential.

Called to Learn

Learning is an ongoing activity. Since God has created us in His image and redeemed us by the sacrifice of Christ, He calls us to a life of constant growth and fruitfulness. Ignorance produces sterility. Apathy creates stagnancy. God's approval of our faithfulness in stewardship is commensurate with our diligence in fulfilling responsibilities. "Study to shew thyself approved unto God," Paul says, ever fond of the scholar's metaphor (2 Timothy 2:15). Diligence, discipline, informed inquiry, and purposeful pursuit of understanding form essential parts of mature Christian development. God entrusts us with increased capacity as we exercise ourselves unto godliness (1 Timothy 4:7).

Christians serious about their faith will resist indolence. The adventurous quest for expanded truth about God and His creation will summon us to study. If a mind is a serious thing to waste (as the slogan tells us), then Christians dare not neglect their minds. But if we restrict Christian learning to the "intellect," we make a grave error. God has challenged us to acquire skills and refine the ones we have. Whatever our calling, we should strive to become more proficient and enhance our gifts. One young man approached Dan Crawford, missionary to Africa, and told Crawford he would give everything to know the Bible the way Crawford knew it. "That's just what I gave," Crawford replied.

Spiritual growth requires study and education as well as prayer and fellowship, and Christians must learn to develop lifelong habits of study. Often small-group interaction can aid education. The proverb "iron sharpeneth iron . . ." works in education as well as in friendship (Proverbs 27:17). Small group Bible studies, discussion groups, book-review sessions, and informal colloquia of limited focus allow interchange among minds and keep them on the cutting edge. Typically churches have rich resources to sponsor these activities. Sunday sermons and services have an important role but they alone prove inadequate. A complement of educational enterprises appropriate for different abilities, appetites, and interests can contribute to maturity in the Christian life.

Life flourishes in environments abounding with varied arrangements of resources. When challenges require new solutions to problems, creativity occurs. In our lives a dynamic and dialectic tension prompts us to call upon the things we have learned or prods us to learn anew. A strong vigorous Christian life demands that we be about the business of learning. Keen observation of nature and society stimulates sensation, alerting us to the wonders in God's order of creation. When we engage in systematic study in the fields of the arts and sciences, we sharpen our perspective and gain awareness of the ways in which God works and communicates. The life of language (written and spoken) allows us to store learning away for reflection and recall. Memory provides personal biography and permits sequence and a sense of historical continuity. Artistic and expressive imagery touch transcendence, hinting at "something superior to us by every measure of value we know and some that elude us."[11] Because small minds construct "small gods," we would do well to heed the advice of J. B. Phillips and recognize the enormity of the God we worship.[12]

Formal schooling is simply one aspect of learning. Ideally, what we learn in schools should provide us with skills and insights to tie together the vast learning that occurs in everyday life. Admittedly and regrettably, modern society's obsession with specialization has produced fragmentation, and often relationships once readily available to former ages have been lost to ours. God's Word gives Christians a grand perspective of His workings and the interrelationship among them. Through revelation, He has unveiled the grand design. The pieces fit together, and the picture becomes more precise through purposeful and diligent study of all areas of legitimate learning. As active, lifelong learners who "abound more and more," we "please God" (1 Thessalonians 4:1).

Out of curiosity, children quite naturally seem eager to learn, but the surprise of learning and living fades for many Christians, and study becomes a chore they seek to avoid. Laziness, a lack of interest, or limited ambition hinder Christian learning. If eternity will provide a cosmic context for investigation and inquiry,

should not we zealously pursue learning in this life? Future comprehension of the eternal will, I suspect, be in proportion to how
we have developed present capacities. Not only do we learn in
this life for active service here, we can also get a "head start" on
heaven.

Christians plan for so many things in life, but so few seem to
plan their learning. After the days of formal education end, learning becomes random and haphazard. Passive hearing takes the
place of active study. I am encouraged by a select group of
"senior saints" who still engage in daily, diligent study. A woman
in her nineties recently enrolled in a course in New Testament
Greek at a local college. The popularity of Elderhostel programs
for retired people tells us that not everyone remains content to
send his mind on a permanent vacation. But study, beside being
an intellectual exercise, can develop sensitivity and empathy.
New learnings free us from self-preoccupation and help us view
life more grandly and more compassionately. What C. S. Lewis
wrote about reading is equally true of all learning undertaken as
a service to God:

> . . . Though it is not essentially an affectional or
> moral or intellectual activity, it has something in com-
> mon with all three. In love we escape from our self
> into one another. In the moral sphere, every act of
> justice or charity involves putting ourselves in the other
> person's place and thus transcending our own compet-
> itive particularity. In coming to understand anything
> we are rejecting the facts as they are for us in favour
> of the facts as they are. . . . Obviously this process
> can be described either as an enlargement or as a tem-
> porary annihilation of self. But that is an old paradox:
> "he that loseth his life shall save it."[13]

15

PASSING THE TEST

... And with what measure ye mete, it shall be measured to you again.

Matthew 7:2

How do I love thee? Let me count the ways. . . .[1]

As has often been said, measurement is the beginning of science . . . because our ability to predict the behaviour of a phenomenon must remain very restricted until we can measure it. It does not follow, however, that no knowledge whatsoever is possible without measurement. . . .[2]

In a measurement course I teach, I often use an exercise in which I write the number *60* on the blackboard and tell the students a certain student received this score on an examination. I then ask for their reactions. Invariably, I get remarks such as:

"The student failed. Sixty is a failing grade."

"Probably needs some remedial work. A little more help and the student could pass."

"Almost made it but not quite. Student needs to work harder."

"Below average ability."

Reactions to such a score typically involve the naive notion that any score has a predetermined interpretation, and because, during their educational careers, students have learned to associate 70 percent with minimum passing performance, they assume that any number less than that means failure. That's not an uncommon response, but it is an inappropriate one. A multitude of factors go into an interpretation of performance. Before making any evaluation of performance, we must thoroughly consider the basis for it.

The Final Evaluation

All teaching begins with objectives and concludes with evaluation. Without some form of evaluation at some legitimate point in the educational sequence, neither teacher nor student has any way of determining the effectiveness of the instruction. So master-teachers always consider the consequence of their teaching and provide abundant opportunities for students to test themselves.

Testing is implicit in education. We must give students reasonable ways of telling whether they have succeeded. During periods of examination, we subject to scrutiny the effort and energy they have expended. Have students learned anything? Has the teaching been effective? Has the expenditure been worth it?

Examinations assess the worth of any effort. Typically educators define a test as a set of tasks (or items) to be performed. Presumably these tasks represent the learning experiences. If a student has studied mathematics, his teacher may present a set of problems for him to solve. If instructed in playing a musical instrument, the student must have an opportunity to demonstrate her proficiency in that skill. Without such a testing situation, there can be no assurance that learning has happened.

Christ's Testings

Our Lord Jesus Christ was the sinless Son of God. Time and again, He challenged His detractors to demonstrate that He had been guilty of any transgression, but they could bring no accusation against Him (John 8:46). As the very verdict of Pilate echoed: ". . . I find no fault in this man" (Luke 23:4). Yet our Lord was *tested* Himself, "in all points like as we are" (Hebrews 4:15). The tests to which Christ was subjected were not intended principally to see whether He would succumb, but to provide clear and incontrovertible proof that He was who He claimed to be. "Declared to be the Son of God with power," Jesus demonstrated the truth of this declaration "by the resurrection from the dead" (Romans 1:4). The test of the tomb ultimately tested His character and claims! The corpseless crypt was the evidence— the final examination.

Our Lord, the Master-Teacher, did learn from His *earthly* experiences. He did not play some kind of charade, for the amusement of an angelic audience; nor did He work out some slickly choreographed sideshow to dazzle earthlings. Instead He lived His life in full submission and obedience to the Father, and learned lessons as real as any we may experience. Though He was the Son of God, "yet learned he obedience by the things which he suffered" (Hebrews 5:8). He passed every test flawlessly. There was not a defect in His character or a deficiency in His performance. Presented by the devil with the most rigorous, relentless challenges, the Christ of God proved Himself more than a match for them and him. Tested in the wilderness (Luke 4:1–13), Jesus gave all the right answers for the right reasons.

Certain standardized tests used in education contain questions designed to tap consistency of response. If the test taker wants to create a certain impression, he may respond to items in ways he believes will portray him favorably. Clinical personality tests are particularly susceptible to "impression management." To discourage these responses or to identify when that intention has prompted responses, these tests have built-in "lie scales," which alert the examiner to the test taker's bias. Certain items throughout the test can be used to identify inconsistencies and consequently reveal the lack of veracity. Jesus was always perfectly consistent, with never any ambiguity in His responses. His teaching and His life correlated perfectly. His promises and proclamations were always "yea and amen" (*see* 2 Corinthians 1:20).

Measured by the Master

Throughout the Gospels, the Master-Teacher provided His disciple-students with examinations. The testings took various forms, but He always designed and intended them for the students' profit. If they had not achieved mastery, He provided remedial experiences in the areas of deficiency. The Lord will not send His disciples on any mission until they have proven their capabilities. In education we term the type of testing that occurs in the context of learning and that provides immediate feedback for the purpose of correcting errors "formative evaluation." After the teachings of the Sermon on the Mount, the Lord provided tests for His disciples. To determine whether they had understood His claims, He commanded them to go to the "other side" (Matthew 8:18). Would they willingly follow where He would lead them in the new life? A scribe wanted security, and an unnamed disciple wanted some leisure time before he made his commitment (Matthew 8:19–22). Subsequently, a series of events unfolded in which Jesus demonstrated His kingdom claims and gave the disciples time to test themselves on the lessons learned on the Mount. The examinations became progressively more complex. Initially, the tests were little more than opportunities to observe the Master and identify the correctness of His responses to a variety of challenging situations. Peter, particularly, failed his test at the trial of the Lord, but later, on the beach at dawn, replied affirmatively and correctly to the question: "Lovest thou me more than these?" (John 21:15–17).

Evaluations must be conducted carefully and correctly, because unwise and premature assessment can abort the learning process. Like a child who continually uproots the plant to see if it's growing, teachers maniacal about measurement will not give time for the steady growth genuine learning produces. Jesus did nothing before its time. He did not undertake any evaluation before the optimum moment. The theme of "the hour" marks out the beat through the melody of John's Gospel—a steady movement toward the crescendo. Each measure moved with regularity. Perfect cadence. At the marriage of Cana, Christ would serve no wine before its time. His final test would occur not at Cana, but at Calvary. Only on Golgotha could the wine of His efficacious death change to blood. The cross, not the marriage ceremony, was the point of ultimate assessment. Without error He completed the final examination—the summative evaluation, and the last words of the accomplished act sounded: ". . . It is finished . . ." (John 19:30).

"Everything in its time" refers equally to examinations. The basis for examinations in the school of Christ's learning will be according to God's criteria. The apostle Paul was suspicious of evaluations made solely on the basis of man's "relative" standards. Norm-referenced testing (very common in schools) interprets all performance in terms of the *group* that takes the test. Paul would not have allowed this type of testing: "For we dare not make ourselves of the number, or compare ourselves with some that commend themselves: but they measuring themselves by themselves, and comparing themselves among themselves, are not wise. But we will not boast of things without our measure, but according to the measure of the rule which God hath distributed to us . . .'' (2 Corinthians 10:12, 13).

In the spiritual realm, all evaluations must be according to God's standards. Schools find ''criterion-referenced'' testing a more attractive alternative today and now develop tests that measure student performance against a predetermined competency level. Paul prefers this type of assessment. God allows us individually to learn and serve according to the abilities He has given us. He gives five talents to some; to others, two talents; to others, one (Matthew 25:15). Ultimately God will evaluate us according to our abilities and gifts. Standing before the judgment seat of Christ, we will have our works assessed according to the criteria that God has established (Romans 14:10). We should neither boast of our accomplishments nor lament our ineffectiveness, if we compare ourselves with each other. We achieve according to talent and occasion. God's children are not equally gifted, nor do they have similar opportunities. Therefore we should avoid hasty and ill-considered assessment.

The Master-Teacher is a master measurer. At first He measures gains and growth incrementally. Peter, eager to make quantum leaps in learning, was compelled to revise his expectations. Like the child who went to school on opening day and felt surprised that he had to return the following day, Peter had to learn to stay with it. Like Rome, learning is not built in a day. Things of value are not mastered immediately. In more mature years, Peter advises believers to add one thing to another. Increments may seem slow and tedious, but they are sure (2 Peter 1:5). God multiplies His grace to us. Forgiveness, from the divine perspective, is exponential (seventy times seven), but at the human level of learning, it begins with the incremental (seven times) (Matthew 18:22).

Tests are intended to discriminate among test takers. The so-called difficulty index of an item determines who answers it correctly and who does not. Jesus did not eagerly and immediately eliminate the insincere. Instead He gave generous opportunity for loyalties to develop and strengthen. But His teaching would not tolerate the fainthearted. Moments came when He measured faithfulness. For some, like Judas, Christ lovingly extended the evaluation process until the end. He could have cut him off from fellowship at any point, but instead allowed Judas multiple opportunities to affirm his allegiance to the Savior. Betrayal is the ultimate act, for which no remediation exists. Peter's denial was a momentary lapse of loyalty from which he recovered. Judas's decision to betray the Son of God was prompted by the diabolic transformation that perverted him.

In a decade of public-school teaching, I assigned a failing grade to only one student. Although the formative evaluations reflected in periodic report cards carried an occasional F, just once did I give a summative F. I had established one criterion for passing the courses: *effort*. Students simply had to try. The one failing grade was given because in that rare instance I saw no evidence of the slightest effort.

The Master-Teacher had no interest in breeding a band of failures. He did not design His teaching to prescribe unattainable performance levels. Unlike the graduate professor I had years ago for a course in statistics, He was not elitist in His expectations. "I teach only to the top ten-percent of the class," that statistics teacher announced the first day of the term. "The rest of you may profit a little, but be assured, your final grade cannot possibly reflect other than average or subaverage performance. You will soon see that the material we are dealing with will soon separate the men from the boys. Perhaps some of you may want to consider dropping the course before you get in over your heads." Some did!

Jesus has rigorous performance expectations, but He does not preclude participation in His program by some smug, supercilious sense of exalted importance. "If there first be a willing mind, it is accepted according to that a man hath, and not according to that he hath not" was the Master's motto (2 Corinthians 8:12). Attrition would occur as the disinterested, the uncommitted, the lazy learners peeled off into their own worlds of small concerns. The final examination left one hundred and twenty devoted disciples in the upper room on Pentecost (Acts 1:15). They had survived the rigors of the long periods of learning and the times of testing. The evaluation had left its unmistakable stamp of accomplishment upon them. Like finest earthenware subjected to the test of the furnace's purification process, they had emerged with distinction. Like the vessels of the ancient world that withstood such testing, the disciples were marked with *dokimos* (Greek: "approved"). They had demonstrated their value and usefulness. They had been taught by the Master-Teacher and had learned from Him and each now was "a vessel unto honour, sanctified, and meet for the master's use, and prepared unto every good work" (2 Timothy 2:21).

—— Afterword ——
THE LAST WORD
IN TEACHING

. . . Jesus . . . having loved his own which were in the world, he loved them unto the end.

John 13:1

Every love has its own force; and it cannot lie idle in the soul of the lover. Love must draw the soul on. Do you, then, wish to know the character of love? See where it leads.[1]

At the conclusion of a school year, one junior-high teacher asked her students if they had any final words. "We may not see each other again," she reminded them. "We've spent more than one hundred eighty days together, and now the time for separation has come. As you review the year, what comes to your mind? What would you like to say?" A few minutes of awkward silence followed, then several students arose and said things humorous and serious. When they finished, a student asked the teacher: "How about you? What are your last words to us?" Smiling, she breathed deeply and said in a voice on the verge of tears: "I love you."

Love is not only the last word in teaching, but the basis on which it begins. Saying the words "I love you" may not prove a sufficient foundation on which to build a school year's program; a teacher needs to live them out in the ordinary day-to-day class routine. Noted psychologist Bruno Bettelheim cautions against the simplistic notion that mere verbalization can substitute for heartfelt effort. In that sense, as his book title suggests, *Love Is Not Enough.*[2] But a loveless classroom cramps, confines, and deforms. Without love, schools become cages that captivate and shackle. Love liberates! "The salvation of man is through love and in love."[3]

A team of sociologists studied the environmental conditions under which a sample of two hundred culturally and economically deprived boys from an urban center were raised. After examining the meager resources available to the children and the limited opportunities open to them for advancement, the team concluded that the outlook for the boys was dismal. They predicted that only ten percent of the boys would be spared a life of crime and imprisonment. Some years later, they reexamined the boys' lives to check the accuracy of their predictions. To their astonishment, only *four* of the two hundred had been in trouble with the law. Bewildered by their findings, the researchers set out to discover the reason for this "miracle," and their path took them to a retired schoolteacher who had intensely involved herself in the boys' lives.

The team questioned her about her approach to teaching, her methodology, and her curriculum. Had she done anything unusual? Something innovative? Had she used unusual strategies and techniques with the boys? No, she couldn't think of anything out of the ordinary. No, she taught them the way she had taught all her students. She had no explanation. After apologizing for not giving the researchers more help, with a sigh she whispered almost inaudibly: "I sure did *love* those boys."

Probably the love teachers show in their classrooms explains such transformations. Not sentimental words, not "smiley buttons" or grinning faces that leave the hard task of learning untouched, but love that invests itself in the painful process of promoting growth and sticking with students when logic and common sense say, "Give up."

At the beginning of each semester, I distribute information forms to students and use the data to get to know them better. The forms include a space for a "significant statement," and I encourage students to say something personal—something meaningful about themselves. I was stunned by one student's entry. She had written: "I love you!" I didn't have the courage to ask what she meant by that, but I think she was telling me that our teacher-student relationship had reached the "investment stage."

Apart from the love of her teacher, we cannot understand Helen Keller's astounding accomplishments. "I love Helen" was Ann Sullivan's invitation to one child to be part of a miracle. Love makes teachers "miracle workers."

Jesus provided unqualified acceptance and unlimited love for His disciples. His love endured the cross and agonized until the end. The cross is the clear, unambiguous commendation of the love of God (Romans 5:8). When all else fails, the Master's love continues (1 Corinthians 13:8). When life's supports seem so fragile and perilously near collapse, the sustaining love "beareth all things" (1 Corinthians 13:7).

Jesus loved His disciples in the same way His Father loved Him (John 15:9). He enjoyed the uninterrupted realization that He was loved. Never did a dark cloud of doubt obscure the sunshine of His Father's undiminished pleasure: "Thou art my beloved Son; in thee I am well pleased" (Luke 3:22). The hours of heaven's silence, when the Lamb of God hung upon the cross, lacked God's reassuring voice, but not His sustaining love.

Learning will never turn into a series of gleeful successes; disappointments and failures will come. Christians are not free from the fret that failure brings, but they rest in the assurance of Christ's unabated affection. "Greater love hath no man than this, that a man lay down his life for his friends" (John 15:13). Love will keep us at the difficult and often tedious task of learning. We want to "know him" (Philippians 3:10) because "nobody can in any way love that of which he is totally ignorant."[4] Teacher and student together require love, as Augustine realized, and they must "be bound in love to God who is Truth and therefore the source of all teaching and learning."[5]

Teachers make mistakes. Students frequently err. We are, after all, only human. Knowledge alone will not correct mistakes. Skill itself will not prevent all errors, but ". . . love covereth all sins" (Proverbs 10:12). Graduation day is just around the corner. To change Paul's metaphor, let us learn with patience the lesson set before us, looking unto the Master-Teacher who endured the cross (Hebrews 12:1, 2). The line from the hymn says it so well: ". . . Heartaches all ended, schooldays all done; heaven will open, Jesus will come."

NOTES

Introduction: The Good Teacher

1. Kurt F. Leidecker, *Yankee Teacher: The Life of William Torrey Harris* (New York: Philosophical Library, 1964), vii.

2. Peter Gay, ed., *John Locke on Education* (New York: Teachers College, Columbia Univ. Pub., 1964), 26.

3. Warren Wiersbe, *Listening to the Giants* (Chicago: Moody Press, 1980), 153.

4. "A Letter of Gratitude and Indebtedness," Thomas Wolfe, *Unseen Harvests: A Treasury of Teaching,* eds., Claud M. Fuess and Emory S. Basford (New York: Macmillan, 1947), 437–438.

5. Quoted in Robert L. Taylor, *Winston Churchill: An Informal Study of Greatness* (Garden City, N.Y.: Doubleday, 1952), 69.

6. Ibid., 70.

Chapter 1: Call Me Teacher

1. Helen Keller, "Out of the Dark," *Great Teachers: As Portrayed by Those Who Studied Under Them,* ed. Houston Peterson (New York: Vintage Books, 1946), 5.

2. Malcolm Muggeridge, "An Elderly Teacher," *Things Past,* ed. Ian Hunter (New York: William Morrow, 1978), 17–20.

3. Herman Melville, *Moby Dick* (New York: Rinehart, 1953), 1.

4. Kurt Vonnegut, Jr., *Cat's Cradle* (New York: Delacorte Press, 1963), 13.

5. Gilbert Highet, *The Art of Teaching* (New York: Alfred A. Knopf, 1968), 99.

6. Alfred P. Dennis, "Princeton Schoolmaster," *Great Teachers,* 131.

7. Henry Adams, *The Education of Henry Adams* (New York: Houghton Mifflin, 1918), 300.

8. Houston Peterson has assembled such tributes in *Great Teachers*.

9. Peter F. Drucker, *Adventures of a Bystander* (New York: Harper & Row, 1978), 62.

10. Keller, "Out of the Dark," 7.

11. John Stuart Mill, "Unwasted Years," *Great Teachers,* 17.

12. Ibid., 27.

13. Clyde Kilby, "The Creative Logician Speaking," *C. S. Lewis: Speaker and Teacher,* ed. Carolyn Keefe (Grand Rapids, Mich.: Zondervan Pub., 1971), 27.

14. Brian Sibley, *C. S. Lewis in the Shadowlands* (Old Tappan, N.J.: Fleming H. Revell, 1986), 32–33.

15. Sylvia Ashton-Warner. *Teacher* (New York: Simon & Schuster, 1963), 210–211.

16. Quoted in Lawrence Cremin, *The Transformation of the School: Progressivism in American Education* (New York: Vintage Books, 1964), 128–129.

17. Paul Goodman, *Compulsory Mis-education* (New York: Vintage Books, 1962.

18. James Hilton, *Good-bye, Mr. Chips* (New York: Grosset & Dunlap, 1934), 75.

Chapter 2: A Model Student

1. William Wordsworth, "XI Stanzas Suggested in a Steamboat Off Bees' Heads," *The Poetical Works of William Wordsworth* (London: Oxford Univ. Press, 1947), 30.

2. William Wordsworth, *The Prelude,* "Book XIII" ibid., 231–232.

3. James Whitcomb Riley, "Old School-Day Romances," *Unseen Harvests: A Treasury of Teaching,* ed. Claude M. Fuess and Emory S. Basford (New York: Macmillan, 1952), 519.

4. James Jordan, "Playing With the Medium," *The New Teachers,* ed. Don M. Flournoy, et al. (San Francisco: Jossey-Bass, 1972), 44.

5. Charles Dickens, *The Life and Adventures of Nicholas Nickleby* (London: Oxford Univ. Press, 1960), 93.

6. Charlotte Brontë, *Jane Eyre* (New York: Modern Library, 1950), 61.

7. Thomas Hughes, *Tom Brown's School Days* (High School Book League), 94.

8. George Sheehan, *Running and Being* (New York: Simon & Schuster, 1978), 86.

9. Maslow discusses this concept in a number of his works, *see* particularly Abraham H. Maslow, *Motivation and Personality,* 2nd ed. (New York: Harper & Row, 1970).

10. John Dewey, *Schools of Tomorrow* (New York: E. P. Dutton, 1915), 102.

11. Gilbert Highet, *The Art of Teaching* (New York: Alfred A. Knopf, 1968), 260–261.

12. Parker J. Palmer, *To Know as We Are Known: A Spirituality of Education* (New York: Harper & Row, 1983), xi–xiv.

13. Helen Keller, "Out of the Dark," *Great Teachers,* ed. Houston Peterson (New York: Vintage Books, 1946), 11–12.

Chapter 3: The Wonder of the Word

1. Robert Anderson, *Forgotten Truths* (Grand Rapids, Mich.: Kregel Pub., 1980), 6.

2. Christopher Morley, "Quaker Scholar," *Great Teachers,* ed. Houston Peterson (New York: Vintage Books, 1946), 125.

3. Lawrence Cremin, *American Education: The Colonial Experience* (New York: Harper & Row, 1972), 40.

4. Robert Anderson, *Types in Hebrews* (Grand Rapids, Mich.: Kregel Pub., 1978).

5. E. B. Castle, *Ancient Education and Today* (Baltimore: Penguin Books, 1961), 63–64.

6. Jill Morgan, *A Man of the Word* (Grand Rapids, Mich.: Baker Book House, 1972), 26.

7. Ibid., 29.

8. Jerome Bruner, *Toward a Theory of Instruction* (Cambridge, Mass.: Harvard Univ. Press, 1967), 12–13.

9. Geoffrey Bull, *God Holds the Key* (London: Pickering & Inglis, 1959), 116.

Chapter 4: Words of Men

1. William Law, *Christian Perfection,* quoted in *Christianity Today* (July 11, 1986), 43.

2. Charles Kingsley, cited in Charles E. Jones, *The Books You Read* (Harrisburg, Penn.: Executive Books, 1986).

3. Elton Trueblood, *The Teacher* (Nashville, Tenn.: Broadman Press, 1980), 23.

4. *Harrisburg Evening News* (July 14, 1986).

5. Trueblood, *Teacher,* 3.

6. C. S. Lewis, *Surprised by Joy* (New York: Harvest Book, 1955), 113.

7. Cited in Earl Pullias and James Young, *A Teacher Is Many Things* (Bloomington, Ind.: Indiana Univ. Press, 1968), 162.

8. Jones, *The Books You Read.*

9. James Stewart, *A Faith to Proclaim* (Grand Rapids, Mich.: Baker Book House, 1972), 30.

10. Raymond E. Fancher, *Psychoanalytic Psychology: The Development of Freud's Thought* (New York: W. W. Norton, 1973), 7.

11. Miguel de Cervantes, *Don Quixote* (New York: Random House, 1941), 26, 27.

12. Jim Elliot, *Journals of Jim Elliot,* ed. Elisabeth Elliot (Old Tappan, N.J.: Fleming H. Revell, 1978).

13. Howard Taylor and Mary G. Taylor, *Hudson Taylor's Spiritual Secret* (Chicago: Moody Press, 1932), 16–17.

14. Lewis, *Surprised by Joy,* 10.

15. Ibid., 223.

16. Roger L. Green and Walter Hooper, *C. S. Lewis: A Biography* (New York: Harcourt, Brace, Jovanovich, 1974), 44.

17. C. S. Lewis, *God in the Dock,* ed. Walter Hooper (Grand Rapids, Mich.: Eerdmans Pub., 1970), 202.

18. Lewis, *Surprised by Joy,* 191.

19. Stanislav Andreski, *Social Sciences as Sorcery* (New York: St. Martin's Press, 1972), 11.

20. Richard P. Feynman, *Surely You're Joking, Mr. Feynman!* ed. Edward Hutchings (New York: W. W. Norton, 1985), 291–302.

21. John Bunyan, *The Holy War* (Chicago: Moody Press, 1948), 51.

22. Alexander Whyte, *Treasury of Alexander Whyte,* ed. Ralph G. Turnbull (Grand Rapids, Mich.: Baker Book House, 1968), 130.

Chapter 5: Drawing Near

1. Gilbert Highet, *The Immortal Profession* (New York: Weybright & Talley, 1976), 41.

2. John Reque, "After Thirty-One Years in the Classroom," *Education Week* (March 5, 1986), 17.

3. George Bailey, "In the University," *C. S. Lewis: Speaker and Teacher,* ed. Carolyn Keefe (Grand Rapids, Mich.: Zondervan Pub., 1971), 106.

4. For a discussion of the terms, *see* Spiros Zodhiates, *Pursuit of Happiness* (Ridgefield, N.J.: AMG Pub., 1966) 255–280.

5. Ibid., 257.

6. David Ehrenfeld, *The Arrogance of Humanism* (New York: Oxford Univ. Press, 1975), 21.

7. Edward Kuhlman and Howard Landis, "Glimpses of God's Grace in Greece," *Evangelical Visitor* (May 25, 1979), 4–5.

8. Jim Elliot's journal reveals a heart aflame for God. Jim Elliot, *The Journals of Jim Elliot,* ed. Elisabeth Elliot (Old Tappan, N.J.: Fleming H. Revell, 1978), 72.

9. Geoffrey Bull, *The Sky Is Red* (London: Pickering & Inglis, 1965), 123.

Chapter 6: Awakening Potential

1. Haim G. Ginott, *Teacher and Child* (New York: Macmillan, 1972), 256.

2. Ibid., 242.

3. Nikos Kazantzakis, *Report to Greco* (New York: Simon & Schuster, 1965), 494–495.

4. George Sheehan, *Running and Being* (New York: Simon & Schuster, 1978), 27.

5. Victor E. Frankl, *Psychotherapy and Existentialism* (New York: Simon & Schuster, 1968), 8–12.

6. William Glasser, *Positive Addiction* (New York: Harper & Row, 1976), 14.

7. Lawrence J. Crabb, Jr., *Effective Biblical Counseling* (Grand Rapids, Mich.: Zondervan Pub., 1977), 61.

8. Leo Buscaglia has written extensively on the topic of love.

9. Jean Mizer, "Cipher in the Snow," *NEA Journal* (November, 1964), 8–10.

10. Glasser, *Addiction,* 1–31.

11. Skinner's book of two decades ago denied the need for dignity any longer. *See* B. F. Skinner, *Beyond Freedom and Dignity* (New York: Bantam Books, 1972).

12. Jean Jacques Rousseau, *Emile of Jean Jacques Rousseau: Selections,* ed. William Boyd (New York: Teachers College Press, 1962), 74.

13. Philip Phoenix, "Teaching as Celebration," *Excellence in University Teaching* (Columbia, S. C.: Univ. of South Carolina Press, 1975), 26.

Chapter 7: Standing Between

1. Geoffrey Bull, *The Sky Is Red* (London: Pickering & Inglis, 1965), 128.

2. George Morrison, *The Unlighted Lustre* (Grand Rapids, Mich.: Baker Book House, 1971), 71.

3. This is illustrated in the classic social psychology experiment of Ronald Lippitt and R. K. White, "An Experimental Study of Leadership and Group Life," *Readings in Social Psychology* (New York: Holt, Rinehart, & Winston, 1958), 496–511.

4. Marshall McLuhan, *Understanding Media: The Extensions of Man* (New York: Signet Books, 1964), ix and chapter 1.

5. Robert Anderson makes this point emphatically in *Types in Hebrews* (Grand Rapids, Mich.: Kregel Pub., 1978), 26.

6. Martin Buber, *I and Thou,* trans. Walter Kaufman and S. G. Smith (New York: Charles Scribner's Sons, 1970).

7. There is a growing body of literature on this topic. A readable Christian examination of the topic can be found in Edward Kuhlman and Howard Landis, "Believer Burn-out: The Spiritual Exhaustion Syndrome," *Evangelical Visitor* (November 25, 1980).

8. Malcom X, *The Autobiography of Malcom X* (New York: Grove Press, 1964), 37.

9. Ibid., 39.

10. Abraham Maslow, *Motivation and Personality,* 2nd ed. (New York: Harper & Row, 1970).

11. Civilla Martin, "Accepted in the Beloved," Hope Pub., 1930.

12. Sidney Jourard, *The Transparent Self,* rev. ed. (New York: D. Van Nostrand, 1971), 187.

13. Robert Rosenthal and Lenore Jacobson, *Pygmalion in the Classroom* (New York: Holt, Rinehart & Winston, 1968).

14. George Bernard Shaw, *Pygmalion* (New York: Dodd, Mead, 1942).

15. Haim Ginott, *Teacher and Child* (New York: Macmillan, 1972), 315.

16. Jourard, *Transparent Self*, 134–135.

17. Ginott, *Teacher and Child*, 304–305.

18. This domain of learning has been described by David Krathwohl, *Taxonomy of Educational Objectives*, Handbook 2, "Affective Domain" (New York: McKay, 1964).

19. Martin E. Seligman, *Helplessness: On Depression, Development and Death* (San Francisco: W. H. Freeman, 1975).

20. Quoted in Francine Klagsbrun, *Youth and Suicide* (New York: Pocket Books, 1977), 30.

21. William Glasser, *Positive Addiction* (New York: Harper & Row, 1976), 14.

Chapter 8: Coming to a Needy World

1. Haim Ginott, *Teacher and Child* (New York: Macmillan, 1972), 316.

2. Richard Weaver, *Ideas Have Consequences* (Chicago: Univ. of Chicago Press, 1984), 44.

3. The Greek word *eutheos* is found forty times throughout this Gospel.

4. Geoffrey Bull, *The Sky Is Red* (London: Pickering & Inglis, 1965), 143.

5. Robert Anderson, *The Gospel and Its Ministry* (Grand Rapids, Mich.: Kregel Pub., 1978), 7.

6. Corrie ten Boom, *Prison Letters* (Old Tappan, N. J.: Fleming H. Revell, 1975), 28.

7. John Milton, "On His Blindness," *The Pleasures of Poetry*, ed. Donald Hall (New York: Harper & Row, 1971), 114.

8. Edward Le Joly, *Servant of Love* (San Francisco: Harper & Row, 1977), 12–13.

9. I am indebted to Geoffrey Bull's imaginative description of the area. *See* Bull, *The Sky*, chapter 18.

10. Some Bible expositors have suggested that this area was the land inhabited by the three tribes that chose to stay on the other side of the Jordan River.

11. Andrew Bonar, *Memoirs of McCheyne* (Chicago: Moody Press, 1947), 18–22.

12. Ibid., 53–54.

13. Ginott, *Teacher and Child,* 45.

14. Victor Frankl, *Man's Search for Meaning* (New York: Pocket Books, 1959), 6.

15. Edward Kuhlman, "DeCiphered," *The Personnel and Guidance Journal* (May, 1983), 580.

16. Parker Palmer, *To Know as We Are Known: A Spirituality of Education* (New York: Harper & Row, 1983), 8–10.

17. August Van Ryn, *Meditations in Mark* (Neptune, N.J.: Loizeaux Bros., 1957), 66–67.

Chapter 9: Leading the Way

1. John Dewey, *Democracy and Education* (New York: Macmillan, 1922), 21.

2. Nikos Kazantzakis, *The Last Temptation of Christ* (New York: Simon & Schuster, 1966), 4.

3. Haim Ginott, *Teacher and Child* (New York: Macmillan, 1972), 302–303.

4. Ibid., 304.

5. Ibid., 303–304.

6. Edmund Gosse, *Father and Son* (Boston: Houghton Mifflin, 1965).

7. Marshall McLuhan, *Understanding Media: The Extensions of Man* (New York: Signet Books, 1964), ix and chapter 1.

8. *See* A. Bandura, *Social Learning Theory* (Englewood Cliffs, N. J.: Prentice Hall, 1977).

9. Merle Curti, *The Social Ideas of American Educators* (Paterson, N. J.: Littlefield, Adams, 1963), 500–501.

10. Eugene Peterson, *Run With the Horses* (Downers Grove, Ill.: InterVarsity Press, 1983), 11.

11. *See* John Dewey, *Schools of Tomorrow* (New York: E. P. Dutton, 1915). The concept "learn by doing" is associated with this work.

12. E. B. Castle, *Ancient Education and Today* (Baltimore: Penguin Books, 1961), 63–64.

13. H. I. Marrou, *A History of Education in Antiquity* (New York: Mentor Books, 1956).

14. Ibid., 37.

15. Ibid., 92.

Chapter 10: Enlarging the Mystery

1. Walt Whitman, "An Old Man's Thought of School," *Unseen Harvests: A Treasury of Teaching,* ed. Claude M. Fuess and Emory S. Basford (New York: Macmillan, 1952), 212.

2. George Morrison, *Sun-Rise* (Grand Rapids, Mich.: Baker Book House, 1971), 17.

3. William Watson, "World-Strangeness," *The Home Book of Quotations,* ed. Burton Stevenson (New York: Dodd, Mead, 1958), 2242.

4. Alfred Lord Tennyson, *Poetic Works of A. L. Tennyson* (Boston: Houghton Mifflin, 1899), 351.

5. Walter A. Dyer, "Garman of Amherst," *Great Teachers,* ed. Houston Peterson (New York: Vintage Books, 1946), 117–119.

6. George Leonard, *Education and Ecstasy* (New York: Dell Pub., 1968), 5.

7. William I. Thompson, *Darkness and Scattered Light* (New York: Anchor Books, 1978), 110.

8. George Morrison, "The Reawakening of Mysticism," *Morning Sermons* (Grand Rapids, Mich.: Baker Book House, 1971), 3.

9. Ian Hunter, *Malcolm Muggeridge: A Life* (Nashville, Tenn.: Thomas Nelson, 1980), 12.

10. C. S. Lewis, *The Problem of Pain* (New York: Macmillan, 1962), especially chapters 1, 2.

11. Peter Bien, "Metaphysics, Myth and Politics," *Excellence in University Teaching* (Columbia, S.C.: Univ. of South Carolina Press, 1975), 170.

12. Morrison, "Reawakening," 7.

13. Ibid., 11.

14. Edith Schaeffer has written extensively, and *L'Abri* describes the ministry in Switzerland.

15. Jacques Ellul, *The Technological Society* (New York: Vintage Books, 1967), 349.

16. Alexander Whyte, *Treasury of Alexander Whyte,* ed. Ralph G. Turnbull (Grand Rapids, Mich.: Baker Book House, 1968), 177.

17. The writings of A. W. Tozer are replete with references to the mystic writers. *See especially* David J. Fant, *A. W. Tozer: A Twentieth Century Prophet* (Harrisburg, Penn.: Christian Pub., 1964), chapter 4.

18. Morrison, "Reawakening," 4–5.

19. Dyer, "Garman of Amherst," 105.

20. Ibid., 106.

21. Hence the title of his biography, *Surprised by Joy* (New York: Harvest Books, 1955).

22. John Calvin, cited in *St. Augustine on Education*, ed. and trans. George Howie (Chicago: Henry Regnery, 1969), 25.

23. Haim Ginott, *Teacher and Child* (New York: Macmillan, 1972), 310.

24. Ibid., 311.

25. William Blake, "Auguries of Innocence," *The Pleasures of Poetry*, ed. Donald Hall (New York: Harper & Row, 1971), 132–133.

26. Malcolm Muggeridge, *A Third Testament* (Boston: Little, Brown, 1976), 86.

27. Morrison, "Reawakening," 10.

Chapter 11: The Master-Teacher

1. Dickson S. Miller, "Beloved Psychologist," *Great Teacher*, ed. Houston Peterson (New York: Vintage Books, 1946).

2. Rebecca Caudill, *Susan Cornish* (New York: Viking Press, 1956), 60.

3. National Commission on Excellence in Education. *A Nation at Risk: The Imperative for Educational Reform* (Washington, D. C.: United States Department of Education, 1983).

4. Benjamin Bloom, "The Master Teachers," *Phi Delta Kappan* 63 (June, 1982), 664–668, 715.

5. Maxine Greene, "A Philosophical Look at Merit and Mastery in Teaching," *The Elementary School Journal* 86 (September, 1985), 17–25.

6. Ibid.

7. Plato, *The Republic of Plato*, trans. Francis M. Cornford (New York: Oxford Univ. Press, 1945), 190–191.

8. Gilbert Highet, *The Art of Teaching*, (New York: Alfred A. Knopf, 1968), 176.

9. Haim G. Ginott, *Teacher and Child* (New York: MacMillan, 1972), 137.

10. George Morrison, *The Wind on the Heath* (Grand Rapids, Mich.: Baker Book House, 1971), 54.

11. *Charismatic* is used here in the way Max Weber used it to indicate an inherent personal attraction only a handful of people possess. For a discussion, *see* Max Weber, "Bureaucracy," *From Max*

Weber, trans. Hans H. Gerth and C. Wright Mills (New York: Oxford University Press, 1964), 295.

12. George Orwell, *1984* (New York: Harcourt Brace, 1949).

13. Quoted in Geoffrey Bull, *The Sky Is Red* (London: Pickering & Inglis, 1965), 119.

14. Parker J. Palmer, *To Know as We Are Known: A Spirituality of Education* (New York: Harper & Row, 1983), 44.

15. Walter A. Dyer, "Garman of Amherst," *Great Teachers,* 119.

16. William Blake, "Notebook Drafts VI," *The Poems of William Blake,* ed. W. H. Stevenson (New York: W. W. Norton, 1971), 481.

17. Cited in "Mark Hopkins," *Great Teachers,* 75.

18. Roger L. Green and Walter Hooper, *C. S. Lewis: A Biography* (New York: Harcourt, Brace, Jovanovich, 1974), 85.

19. Carolyn Keefe, *C. S. Lewis: Speaker and Teacher,* 174.

20. *Ibid.,* 176–177.

21. Arnold A. Dallimore, *George Whitefield* vol. 1 (Edinburgh: Banner of Truth Trust, 1970), 116.

22. Highet, *Art of Teaching,* 248.

23. Noam Chomsky, *Language and Mind* (New York: Harcourt, Brace, & World, 1968).

24. Lewis Carroll, *Through the Looking Glass* (New York: Bramhall House, 1960), 269.

25. Edwin Newman, *A Civil Tongue* (New York: Warner Books, 1977).

26. *See* John E. Sadler, *J. A. Comenius and the Concept of Universal Education* (New York: Barnes & Noble, 1966).

Chapter 12: Master of the Metaphors

1. William Carlos Williams, "A Sort of a Song," *The Collected Later Poems of William Carlos Williams,* rev. ed. (New York: New Directions Pub., 1950).

2. G. Campbell Morgan, *The Parables and Metaphors of Our Lord* (New York: Fleming H. Revell, 1956), 18.

3. John Ciardi, *How Does a Poem Mean?* Boston: Houghton Mifflin, 1959), 867.

4. Morgan, *Parables and Metaphors,* 14.

5. Plato, *The Republic of Plato,* trans. Francis M. Cornford (New York: Oxford Univ. Press, 1945), chapter 25.

6. Alexander Pope, *An Essay on Criticism,* "Part II," *The Pleasures of Poetry,* ed. Donald Hall (New York: Harper & Row, 1971), 118.

7. R. C. Trench, *Notes on the Parables of Our Lord* (Grand Rapids, Mich.: Baker Book House, 1948), 11.

8. Ibid., 8.

9. The single most comprehensive treatment of the figures of speech in the Bible is E. L. Bullinger, *Figures of Speech in the Bible* (Grand Rapids, Mich.: Baker Book House, 1968).

10. Derek Kidner, *Proverbs* (Downers Grove, Ill.: InterVarsity Press, 1976), 28.

Chapter 13: The Master Lesson

1. George Morrison, *Morning Sermons* (Grand Rapids, Mich.: Baker Book House, 1971), 165–170.

2. Geoffrey Bull, *The Sky Is Red* (London: Pickering & Inglis, 1965), 117.

3. F. B. Meyer, *The Directory of the Devout Life* (Old Tappan, N.J.: Fleming H. Revell, 1904), 10–11.

4. Gilbert Highet, *The Art of Teaching* (New York: Alfred A. Knopf, 1968), 193.

5. Victor Frankl, *Man's Search for Meaning* (New York: Pocket Books, 1959), 641.

6. Helen Keller, "Out of the Dark," *Great Teachers,* ed. Houston Peterson (New York: Vintage Books, 1946), 6.

7. Bull, *The Sky,* 120.

8. Highet, *Art of Teaching,* 63.

9. Bull, *The Sky,* 137.

10. Ibid.

11. Elton Trueblood, *The Teacher* (Nashville, Tenn.: Broadman Press, 1980), 78.

Chapter 14: God's Truth Is All Truth

1. William Wordsworth, "The Prelude," *The Poetical Works of William Wordsworth* (London: Oxford Univ. Press, 1947), 45.

2. John Dewey, *Democracy and Education* (New York: Macmillan, 1922), 89–90.

3. Quoted in Houston Smith, *Beyond the Post-Modern Mind* (New York: Crossroad Pub., 1982), 6.

4. Herman H. Horne, "Idealism in Education," ed. Joe Parks, *The Philosophy of Education* (New York: Macmillan, 1963), 237.

5. St. Augustine, *St. Augustine on Education*, ed. and trans. George Howie (Chicago: Henry Regnery, 1969), 5.

6. Ibid., 18.

7. Arthur F. Holmes, *The Idea of a Christian College* (Grand Rapids, Mich.: William Eerdmans Pub., 1975), 43.

8. Ibid., 44.

9. Peter Gay, *The Enlightenment: An Interpretation* (New York: Vintage Books, 1968), 10.

10. Holmes, *Christian College*, 23.

11. Smith, *Post-Modern Mind*, 114.

12. J. B. Phillips, *Your God is Too Small*.

13. Quoted in Michael D. Aeschliman, *The Restitution of Man* (Grand Rapids, Mich: William Eerdmans Pub., 1983), 68.

Chapter 15: Passing the Test

1. Elizabeth Barrett Browning, "Sonnets From the Portugese," *The Poetical Works of Elizabeth B. Browning* (New York: Houghton Mifflin, 1974), 223.

2. Stanislav Andreski, *Social Sciences as Sorcery* (New York: St. Martins, 1972), 123.

Afterword: The Last Word

1. Augustine, cited in Robert Meagher, *Augustine: An Introduction* (New York: Harper & Row, 1978), 102.

2. Bruno Bettelheim, *Love Is Not Enough* (Glencoe, Ill.: Free Press, 1950).

3. Victor Frankl, *Man's Search for Meaning* (New York: Pocket Books, 1959), 59.

4. Augustine, *St. Augustine on Education*, ed. and trans. George Howie (Chicago: Henry Regnery, 1969), 109.

5. *Ibid.*, 13.